BETWEEN REALITIES AND IDEALS

FLORIN LEONTE
BETWEEN REALITIES AND IDEALS
Writing the Reform in Franciscan Observant Chronicles

© Palacký University Olomouc, 2025

This book is published under a Creative Commons Attribution-NonCommercial-NoDerivatives 4.0 International License (**CC BY-NC-ND 4.0**). This license does not apply to content that is attributed to sources other than the copyright holder mentioned above. Under this license you are free to share this work, provided the makers are attributed. Its content cannot be used for commercial purposes nor is it allowed to make adaptations without permission from the copyright holder.

For more information about our licenses, please visit https://www.sidestone.com/publishing/creative-commons.

Published by Sidestone Press, Leiden
www.sidestone.com
E-mail: info @ sidestone.nl
Phone: (+31)(0)71-7370131

Layout & cover design: Sidestone Press
Cover image: Medieval gate ornaments, München (photo by Tim Hüfner, unsplash.com)

ISBN 978-94-6426-379-4 (softcover)
ISBN 978-94-6426-380-0 (hardcover)
ISBN 978-94-6426-381-7 (PDF e-book)

DOI: 10.59641/f6i2c3d4e5

This book was written with the financial support of the Czech Science Foundation (GA ČR), under the GA ČR EXPRO project no. 20-08389X, Observance reconsidered: Uses and abuses of the reform (individuals, institutions, society).

Palacký University Olomouc

Contents

Introduction ... 7
   Sources and scope of the present study ... 10
   Argument ... 14
   Method and concepts ... 15

I The Franciscan Observance: Development and Ideals ... 17
   I.1. The emergence of Observance ... 19
   I.2. The pillars of Observance ... 23
   I.3. Medieval discourses of virtues and reform ... 24
   I.4. Observant modulations of the medieval system of moral virtues ... 28
   I.5. The Observants and the medieval discourses of power ... 34

II The Observant Discourse of Reform: Legitimation, Education, and Communication ... 39
   II.1. The Observants and their efforts at institutional legitimation ... 43
   II.2. Integrating education in the Observant discourse of reform ... 46
      II.2.1. Late medieval ideas of education ... 47
      II.2.2. Between devotion and education ... 54
      II.2.3. Observant mentors: Bernardino of Siena, John Capistrano, and their educational activities ... 56
      II.2.4. Education and humanism ... 66
   II.3. Communicating the Observant reform ... 71
      II.3.1. Communication oriented towards moralization: preaching and life-writing ... 72
      II.3.2. Communication for legitimization purposes: documents and letters ... 75
   Conclusion ... 78

III Observant Identity and its Chronicle Forms	**81**
III.1. Authorial fashioning	85
III.2. Narrating Franciscan institutional recognition and religious authority	87
III.3. The Observants as viewed in the chronicles	94
III.4. Ideals in the formation of Observant identity: from spiritual models to political power	97
III.5. Balancing ideals and pragmatism	101
III.6. Otherness	102
III.6.1 The Other: Greeks, Tatars, and Turks	104
III.7. Narrative strategies in the formation of Observant identity	113
III.7.1. Types of chronicle narratives	117
III.7.2. Narrative of events: from leadership-centered episodes to miracles	118
III.7.3. Narrative of conflicts	124
III.7.4. Biographies	128
III.7.5. Observant history: a dynamic enterprise and a story of continuity	134
Conclusion. Narrative Constructions of Observant Identity: Between Action and Ideals	**137**
Bibliography	**141**

Introduction[1]

The Franciscan Observance held a distinct place in the spectrum of late medieval religious transformations.[2] The movement's literary output, spanning diverse genres like sermons, letters, chronicles, or hagiographies, reflected the convergence of transregional political conflicts, theological debates, and practices of popular devotion. By seeking to realign with the original Franciscan ideals of poverty and humility,[3] the Observants called for reform in monastic customs[4] while adapting their own written communication and attitudes in response to questions of religious practices, education,[5] and the Church's authority in the world at the turn of the fifteenth century.[6]

Paramount among the Observants' preoccupations was the control and adaptation of language to various audiences.[7] This concern presented challenges and opportunities for the movement's development, since the Observants pursued the goal of reforming both the monastic environment and the public spirituality. Scholars like Clare Lappin have analyzed in depth Observant literature, including constitutions, hagiographies, and

---

1 This book was written with the generous support of the Czech Science Foundation in the framework of the project: *Observance Reconsidered: The Uses and Abuses of the Reform (Individuals, Institutions, Society)* GX 20-08389X (2020–2024, GAČR EXPRO).
2 See for instance Moorman (1968), who provides a comprehensive overview of the Franciscan Order's development, including the rise of the Observant movement.
3 Several studies have focused on the Observants' interpretation of Franciscan poverty. See Mixson (2009).
4 On insights into the specific reforms advocated by the Observants and how these related to broader trends in monastic reform see Nimmo (1987).
5 For the Franciscan approach to education and learning see Şenocak (2012).
6 See Melville (2016). Thomas Izbicki's studies also provide broader context on the relationship between monastic reform movements and debates about the Church's authority in the late medieval period. See Izbicki (2008a).
7 Roest (2004) and especially Lappin (2000) who explores the use of various discursive tools.

polemics, to understand the group's developing self-image and identity. This involved a shift from a strict, eremitical lifestyle to an active preaching role, creating internal tensions and conflicts with the Conventual Franciscans.[8] The changing relation between texts and contexts, between the articulation of the Franciscans' intentions and the political, economic, or social realities, requires us to examine their discourse on reforming the Church and society. The Observants did not configure such a discourse as a mere epiphenomenon of spiritual practices or socio-political acts, but configured it as a tool of religious and political change that showed regional nuances and occasional contradictions in the process of the Franciscan Observance's expansion. Their linguistic adaptations emerge in the articulation of their constitutions, which reflect a shift towards a centralized and systematized form of religious life.[9] Furthermore, the efforts to control and adapt language also extended to the realm of education, as they sought to provide new recruits with a standardized and rigorous spiritual formation.[10]

Within the Observants' discursive toolbox, narratives in the form of chronicles operated at multiple levels.[11] They served as both records of events in the life of the Franciscan Observants across various geographic areas and as tools shaping the identity, authority, and legacy of themselves or of the individuals and the groups with whom they came into contact. They reinforced the order's place within the Church, offered models of holiness, and forged a shared history for the Observant audience. More intimately, in their composition and purpose, Observant chronicles revealed deliberate acts of collective self-fashioning to shape how the order and its personalities were perceived. To a certain extent, this self-representation echoed the literary strategies of other contemporary movements like the Humanism.[12] For example, the Observants drew on humanist ideas and practices, such as the emphasis on classical learning and eloquence, to enhance their preaching and writing. However, the Observants' relationship with Humanism was not without its tensions, as several humanists critiqued the perceived excesses and religiosity of the Observant movement.

---

8   For perspectives on how the Observants used texts to shape their identity and pursue their reformist goals, see Lappin (2000).
9   Mixson (2015b), 75.
10 Mixson (2015b), 77.
11 See van Houts (1995).
12 Mixson and Roest (2015).

The chronicles offer distinct perspectives on Church history, education, and public morality, functioning as tools of social transformation, in tune with their audiences, primarily monastic readers.[13] Their continuous highlighting of the efforts to advance religious reform signals the engagement with late medieval ethics and political thought. The chronicles prove the Observants' attempts to anchor their spiritual identity into forms of writing and extend their influence in a changing world, acting as models of stability and knowledge. However, as the same chronicles suggest, the project of reform was fraught with tensions, since the different voices within the Order, each with individual perspectives and agendas, often clashed. In this respect, the chronicles recount the efforts of popular figures like John Capistrano or Bernardino of Siena, who preached against heresy and sought to revitalize monastic life. The accounts of various church councils like the one in Constance in early fifteenth century show a commitment to resolving schisms and addressing the growing popularity of various movements like Hussitism. To that extent, we distinguish two main kinds of chronicles: while some emphasize the sanctity and miraculous deeds of its early leaders, thereby reinforcing the Order's spiritual legitimacy, others focus more on the Order's involvement in regional political transactions.[14]

The recent decades have seen studies on a variety of aspects of the Franciscan Observance, from its roots to the influence on later reforms. Scholars have recognized the need to investigate the Observant Reform through the lens of late medieval intellectual history, as evidenced by several recent works. Bert Roest's *A History of Franciscan Education (c. 1210-1517)* gives a comprehensive overview of Franciscan educational practices, including those of the Observants, demonstrating their engagement with late medieval intellectual currents. While focusing on an earlier period, Neslihan Şenocak's monograph, *The Poor and the Perfect: The Rise of Learning in the Franciscan Order, 1209-1310,* lays the groundwork for understanding the intellectual foundations upon which the Observant movement built its claims. Ludovic Viallet's *Les sens de l'observance* examines the Observant movement in Central Europe, paying attention to its intellectual dimensions and their intersection with late medieval reform thought. Letizia Pellegrini argued in favor of a multifaceted Franciscan Observance, whereas a recent scholarly strand

---

13 Roest (2004).
14 Lappin (2000).

examines its Central European variations.[15] Other scholars looked at the historical impact of Observant personalities like John Capistrano and analyze the tensions with the Hussites and other political figures.[16] Research on sermons offered case studies in how Observant thinkers engaged with and reinterpreted earlier Franciscan intellectual traditions.[17] In addition, new scholarly editions of sources like letters and chronicles related to the Observant history facilitated much more informed approaches.[18]

These scholarly works paved the way for a nuanced understanding of the Observant movement's intellectual foundations and key individual movers. They set the stage for further investigations into how the Observants articulated and disseminated their spiritual ideals through various mediums, be they letters, sermons, official proclamations, or narratives. Building upon these results, the present study of two chronicles compiled in the Observant circles with their detailed accounts of devotion practices, mobility patterns, biographies, and narratives of events can yield insights into how they constructed and projected their spirituality. The study of the Observant reform requires therefore not only a scrutiny of its geographical expansion and political connections across Europe, but also an analysis of issues such as language use, communication strategies, and the role of education in the configuration of its identity as reforming group.

Sources and scope of the present study

In particular, the present research aims at exploring the discourse of reform that crystallized among Franciscan Observants in the late medieval period, spanning from its beginnings to the mid-fifteenth century. Given the extensive scope of this topic, it would be impossible to cover the diverse discourse strategies employed by the Observants within the confines of this study. Instead, I will focus on two representative chronicles: the *Chronica ordinis minorum observantum* by Nicolaus Glassberger (c. 1450-1508) and the shorter *Chronica fratrum minorum observantiae* by Bernardino Aquillano (1421-1503), which both offer a historical perspective on the development and spread of the Observant movement. These works not only document the key events and figures of the reform but also reveal the Observants' self-perception and efforts to legitimize their status within changing ecclesiastical and political

---

15 Pellegrini (2018).
16 Kalous & Stejskal (2020) and Pellegrini (2017).
17 See the studies in Muessig (2002) and Pellegrini (2011).
18 E.g. the letters of Capistrano related to the history of Poland. See Kras et alii (2018). Editions of letters and chronicles concerning Capistrano and the Czech lands are under preparation.

milieux. By focusing on narratives, the present study aims at shedding light on the themes, strategies, and objectives of the Observant discourse of reform as they took shape in this genre. The kind of history cultivated by the Observant chroniclers conceived of the Observant reform as a mix of political acts and spiritual exemplarity predicated upon moralization and miraculous events that echoed the profile of the Observance's forefathers. Furthermore, the discourse of reform encapsulated in the narratives was far from uniform but held regional variations determined either by the historical and ecclesiastical context or by the authorial strategies of presenting the Observant reform.

The primary focus here will thus be on the tradition of monastic order chronicles, texts written under the authority of a monastic leader.[19] Like other order chronicles, these narratives were heterogenous in content and structure. Most of them followed a chronological order and included digressions on various topics like general aspects of church history, political events, wars, biographies of prominent individuals, anecdotes, papal bulls, and letters with implications for the order. Often, they embedded local narratives relevant for the history of an order.[20] They also included sections on masters general and other figures, reflecting the interconnectedness of different hierarchical levels within the order. Among the chronicles dealing with the rise and growth of the Franciscan Observance, those of Bernardino Aquilano and Nicholas Glassberger provide detailed illustrations of the order's operations at both spiritual and political levels. If Aquilano's chronicle concentrates on the beginnings and development of the Observance in Italy, Glassberger takes a different approach and proceeds from the early Franciscan history before moving to the Order's life beyond the Alps and its missionary activities in distant Oriental territories.[21] To be sure, these texts were not the only Franciscan Observant narratives. Other monastic chronicles of the order like those by Mariano da Firenze, John of Komorowo, Michael of Carinthia, or Eberhard Ablauff together with a long series of hagiographical compositions dedicated to the personalities

---

19 On the role of abbatial authority in the writing of history, see Pohl (2023).
20 On monastic order chronicles, see Hujbers (2018): 35-142.
21 On Bernardino see Romagnoli (2011) and Pellegrini (2021). On Glassberger see Seton (1923).

of Observance reflected similar concerns and constructed similar models even if they emphasize certain thematic or local variations.[22]

The authors of the narratives had strong ties with the Observant movement. Born in Olomouc, Nicholas Glassberger (1450-1508), studied in Leipzig, and lived for a while in Amberg where he joined the Observance.[23] In 1483 he moved to Nuremberg where he lived until his death. In composing the text, Glassberger had access to the archives, manuscripts, and documents present in the monasteries where he lived as a copyist. Contemporaries recognized him as a trusted repository of older sources.[24] Given his interest in books and learning, he came into contact with the rich families of Nuremberg and the Humanists who lived in South Germany at the end of the fifteenth century. He was a confessor to Caritas Pirckheimer, herself a learned abbess in Nuremberg who appreciated Humanist scholarship inasmuch as she valued monastic life.[25] Even if we do not know details about his career, circumstantial evidence about intellectual life in Southern Germany and his texts show his wide interests and knowledge including history, politics, geography, or scholastic philosophy.[26] As it appears from the sources, in the fifteenth-century, Nuremberg became a center for the study of history and literature. The manuscript catalogue of the Franciscans' library records both religious authors like Saint Augustine or Gregory the Great and classical texts like Seneca's *Letters*, Ovid's *Metamorphoses*, or Sallust's historical narratives.[27] Without doubt, activities like copying manuscripts in convents which contributed to the intellectual life of the city, influenced the Observant movement as well.[28]

Glassberger's chronicle covers the early history of the Franciscan Order from its foundation by Saint Francis in the early thirteenth century through the late fifteenth century. It recounts key events, conflicts, and personalities that shaped the order's development, with a focus on upholding strict observance of the Franciscan Rule. Its major sections and themes include: the life and ministry of Saint Francis; the first generations

---

22 See Lappin (2000) on Mariano da Firenze, John of Komorowo, Michael of Carinthia and Eberhard Ablauff. Ablauff wrote the oldest narrative of the Franciscans in the Bohemian lands, *De novella plantatione provincie Austrie, Bohemie et Polonie, quo ad fratres minores de observantia Cronica* (1505). It served as a source for Michael of Carinthia's more extensive *Chronica Fratrum minorum de Observancia provincie Bohemie*. See Kalous & Stejskal (2020) and Hlaváček (2005).
23 Seton (1923), ix. See also the new editions of Ablauff (2024).
24 Seton (1923), xv.
25 Seton (1923), xvi.
26 Seton (1923), xvi.
27 Seton (1923), 20.
28 Strauss (1977).

of Franciscans and the early expansion of the order; ongoing debates about interpreting poverty and the Rule; establishing the Poor Clares and Third Order Missions beyond Italy and martyrdoms of friars; succession of Ministers General and administration of the order; influential friars, scholars, and conflicts at the University of Paris; interventions by Popes, cardinals, and the Apostolic See. Glassberger emphasizes the important moments from the history of the Franciscans by documenting the early missions to Germany and the difficulties encountered there by the friars. This narrative helps to provide a comprehensive understanding of the Order's development and the challenges it faced in its early years.[29]

The other chronicle discussed here, by Bernardino Aquilano, holds several particular traits as well, since it primarily follows the events occurring in late medieval Italy. Like Glassberger, he begins by detailing the motivations for writing and comments on his method and sources. Aquilano traces the development of the Observant Franciscan movement, beginning with early reform attempts by several anonymous "good friars" and by Angelo de Monte Leone, Angelo Clareno, and the Spirituals. He then focuses on other personalities, detailing their background and impact on the early spread of the movement. The narrative continues with the growth of the Observant movement in Italy, including the expulsion of heretics from Perugia, establishing Observant communities there, and their spread to other provinces. Bernardino highlights notable early Observant friars such as Anthony of Stroncone, before discussing the rise of Observant preaching through figures like Bernardino of Siena and John Capistrano. The text then covers attempts at order-wide reform under Popes Martin V (1417-1431) and Eugene IV (1431-1447). Bernardino Aquilano details the new governance structure for Observants established by Eugene IV's bulls, their separation from Conventuals, and the appointment of Observant Vicars. He recounts conflicts with heretics and Conventuals, including disputes over Eugene's bulls, the controversy surrounding Roberto da Lecce, and struggles in the Roman Curia under Pope Nicholas V (1447-1455). The narrative progresses through the papacy of Callixtus III, John Capistrano's later activities, and further developments pertaining to the Observance under Pope Pius II (1458-1464), born Enea Silvio Piccolomini. Bernardino only briefly addresses provincial matters such as creating the Province of Saint Bernardino of Siena and conflicts in the Balkans which Glassberger treated in detail. The text includes biographical

---

29 Glassberger, *Chronicle*, 11.

sketches of notable Observant friars from various provinces, focusing on their miracles and holy lives.

Because the two chronicles engage with spiritual and political themes, questions arise about how their authors understood Observant reformist identity and how they reflected or modulated it in narrative form. The first section of the study will set the historical and intellectual background of this exploration by focusing on aspects of the development of the Observance relevant to its discourse of reform: origins, growth, protagonists, and the main ideas that shaped the Observants' actions. The second section will elaborate on two areas relevant for the Observant movement: its legitimation in relation to various authorities and their outlook and practices of education. The third part will explore the specific means of communication and dissemination of the Observant message, in particular letters, decrees, and sermons. These sections will be illustrated with examples from the chronicles to understand how narratives responded to the development, actions, and commitments of the Observant movement. In the last section I will move closer to the chronicles and will examine their use of event narratives, biographies, and other sources like sermons or letters. This will help us evaluate the Observants' narrative fashioning of themselves vis-à-vis other Franciscan groups, the authorities, and other religious and ethnic communities with which they came into contact. Each chapter will correlate issues of historical background and the efforts to change the public perception of Franciscan Observance. The relations between individuals, groups, and narrative themes will be examined, with language understood to encompass both choices of form and themes of content. All in all, the present study will consider both continuities and disruptions throughout the order's history.

Argument

The argument of the present study is that the Observants employed narratives equally as historical documents and as instruments for legitimizing their reformist identity, by promoting a vision of continuity and stability. These efforts attended to the intellectual and historical conditions of the late medieval world, including the currents that opposed the Observance. In particular, as depositories of substantial amounts of information, the chronicles made up a kind of monastic *specula* for the Observant congregations to understand the official stance regarding the events and controversies out of which the movement emerged. On the one hand, the narratives show the Observants holding a keen interest in reclaiming their order's recent history, beginning with the life and figure of Francis of Assisi. Each event, example, and celebration in the order's life was recorded to reconstruct the history of the Observance and provide models of exemplary conduct. The chronicles present recovering the past as a necessary process of historical and geographical mapping of religious experiences in relation to their political, social, or cultural contexts. As a means of collective self-presentation, the chronicles shaped the Observant movement's identity by accentuating their distinctive traits from other religious orders. Stories and biographies reinterpreted the past in a moralizing framework and expressed social distance from other groups like the Conventuals. At the same time, the chroniclers bridged the temporal distance between past and present to construct a sense of continuity with popular religious groups and influential personalities.

Paradoxically, while constructing the Order's identity, Observant chronicles also conveyed a sense of fragmentation because of the multitude of participants (members of the monastic orders, popes, rulers, or local governors), events occurring across distant regions, source materials (archives, letters, legends, etc), and themes (religious and lay). This apparent discontinuity stemmed from the chroniclers' ambition to encompass a wide range of information, intended to confer a high epistemological status to their narratives. By presenting a comprehensive and nuanced view of the Order's history, the chronicles achieved a sense of authority and credibility distinct from other genres such as sermons or letters.[30] This high status held significance both within the restricted monastic communities and later for the general public as well.

Method and concepts

Given the multitude of information incorporated in these texts, the study of Observant Franciscan chronicles requires a methodological framework that integrates the close readings of the sources with contextual research to evaluate the effectiveness of chronicles as tools of religious reform. This approach aligns with recent scholarly work on late medieval religious reform movements, where institutional narratives have proven crucial in understanding the construction of religious identities. For instance, Anne Huijbers's work on Dominican chronicles shows how historical and biographical texts accompanied by a change in the idea of authorship served as vehicles for articulating and promoting reform ideals within

---

30   Roest (1997).

religious orders.[31] Like their Dominican counterparts, Franciscan Observant chronicles operated within the medieval historiographical traditions while developing distinct narrative strategies and preferences for themes of involvement with political institutions or conflict resolution.

One path is to examine the language and themes used in the Observants' self-perception and reformist identity, focusing on representing key Observant ideals such as poverty and humility. The present analysis will extend to examining the didactic aims and communication strategies within these narratives, investigating how they sought to educate and influence both monastic and lay audiences through moral teachings and narrative techniques. Central to this approach is discourse analysis, which provides a framework for exploring the *discourse of reform* that permeates these texts. By examining how narrative language constructs meaning, shapes perceptions, and influences social practices, we can uncover the underlying structures, assumptions, and power dynamics that informed the Observants' reformist ideology. The concept of a *discourse of reform*, which I will use here, encompasses not only explicit arguments for change but also implicit ways in which the Observants framed their identity, goals, and relationship to the broader Church and society. This approach follows a growing scholarly recognition that Franciscan institutional narratives, far from being mere repositories of facts, operated as tools for identity formation and reform promotion.[32] It allows us to analyze how they used linguistic and narrative strategies to legitimize their reform efforts and create a distinct spiritual and social identity. This approach will consider the impact of interactions with other religious movements and secular power brokers to address the challenges posed by the geographical dispersion and local expressions of the Observant reform. Thus, by focusing on the reflections of the discourse of reform in chronicles, it becomes possible to identify recurring themes and narratives that shaped the Observants' vision, revealing the assumptions and goals of their reform agenda. To do so, I will deal with illustrative samples from the chronicles of Glassberger and Aquilano, rather than attempting to cover the entire corpus of Observant chronicles which would exceed the scope of this study.

---

31   Hujbers (2018).
32   Hujbers (2018).

I

The Franciscan Observance: Development and Ideals

The first step in this exploration of Observant identity through the lens of narrative chronicles is to examine the beginning and development of the Franciscan Observance. As a movement that arose in response to the widespread yearning for a spiritual way of life, the Observance emphasized a return to the ideals of poverty and spiritual purity championed by Saint Francis. This idea manifested in various ways ever since the emergence of the Franciscan Observance and through upheavals and changes that marked its trajectory and consolidation. The reformist spirit that fueled the Franciscan Observance movement found resonance in the efforts to address the Church's challenges, as exemplified by the actions of numerous popes. In the first half of the fifteenth century, the Observance became a preoccupation of Pope Martin V (1417-1431) who sought to solve internal divisions through initiatives focused on church unity, defense against heresies, and institutional reform.[33] During this period, the Council of Constance (1414-1418) which convened to resolve the Western Schism, that had divided the Church for decades, took into consideration the reality and matters of Franciscan Observance.[34] A few decades later, as the papacy actively integrated the Observance into its efforts of renewal, Pope Eugene IV granted the Observants autonomy within the Franciscan order in 1446, recognizing its growing influence.[35]

Yet, if papal decisions and councils had an impact on the movement's institutional organization, the development of the Observance was a

---

33   Viallet (2013), 33-51.
34   Nimmo (1977), 159-173.
35   Pellegrini (2018).

decentralized process, influenced by the contexts of various territories and communities in Italy or beyond the Alps. The movement adapted to political and regional contexts in which Observant communities operated. The expansion of urban centers and the need for systematic moral instruction led to the emergence of two distinct branches within the Observance: *sub vicariis*, which favored a strict adherence to the rule of Saint Francis, and *sub ministris*, which allowed for certain mitigations in terms of conduct and practices. This division was evident in cities like Florence, where the Observant friars of San Salvatore al Monte represented a faction with a more austere way of life than other groups, while those of Santa Croce embodied a moderate approach.[36]

The Observance responded to late medieval political and social phenomena, such as the conflicts between regional secular authorities or the impact of urbanization. As the movement spread across far and wide geographical areas, it underwent transformations, with several monastic centers shaping its identity, devotion practices, and ideas of sanctity. The shift from the simplicity of the earlier groups of contemplative *fraticelli* to the needs of urban communities necessitated an educated group of friars, further influencing the form and content of the texts produced by the Observants.[37] This shift is clear in the works of the Observant friar James of the Marches, who wrote on preaching and moral theology, addressing the concerns of both religious and lay audiences in a growing urban life. Glassberger's chronicle abundantly illustrates this effort to understand the history of the early Franciscan Order and the role of individual friars in specific events. His chronicle does not focus only on early events and problems like the challenges faced by the Order during Saint Francis' time, including internal conflicts, external threats, or the need for organizational structure.[38] He takes a step forward and explores Observance against the backdrop of the Western Schism (1378-1417), a crisis that not only divided the Church in terms of political allegiances but also had a profound impact on Christians across Europe. His efforts were geared towards a comprehensive account by reproducing documents circulated during the Council of Pisa in 1409, which reflected the frustration and anger that many clerics experienced during this tumultuous period.[39] Aquilano's chronicle also portrays how the Observants navigated the complex political

---

36   Vialet (2016).
37   Vialet (2014) and Tsougarakis (2018).
38   Glassberger, *Chronicle*, 17.
39   Glassberger, *Chronicle*, 229-232.

and social landscape of their time. His account reveals their strategy of engaging with urban populations and secular authorities to advance their reform agenda. Particularly telling is his description of the Observants' establishment in Perugia, where they appealed to civic aspirations for religious reform while positioning themselves against the Conventuals.[40] The chronicle also praises the Observants' political acumen in cultivating relationships with influential figures at the papal curia such as Pietro Noceto, and their use of papal bulls to secure institutional autonomy.[41] These embedded narratives not only documented historical events but also demonstrated how the Observants operated within both ecclesiastical and secular spheres to achieve their reformist goals.

I.1. The emergence of Observance

Several social and political determinants fueled the emergence and expansion of Franciscan Observance in the late medieval period.[42] Contemporary sources, including the chronicles, deplored a decline in the life of mendicant orders, connecting this deterioration to the accelerated economic downturn and the changes in the spiritual life of communities.[43] The aftermath of the Black Death, for instance, led to demographic shifts and economic instability that affected monastic communities. Assertions of property and privilege, along with accommodation to economic and institutional conditions, were correlated with increased mobility and the perceived abandonment of monastic ideals. For example, several Franciscan communities began to accept regular incomes and property ownership, practices that stood in contrast to the order's original commitment to absolute poverty.[44]

The speed and intensity of such changes differed and depended on regional variations. In Italy, where the Observant movement gained momentum earlier and more rapidly than in other parts of Europe, areas experiencing severe economic disruptions saw urgent calls for reform. The response to these challenges varied among religious orders. While the Franciscans responded to questions of property ownership, the Dominicans faced different issues related to their educational mission and involvement in ecclesiastical politics.[45]

---

40 Aquilano, *Chronicle*, 10.
41 Aquilano, *Chronicle*, 50
42 Mixson and Roest (2015).
43 Vauchez (1993), 109-120.
44 Little (1978), 200-215.
45 Nimmo (1987), 150-175.

Other catalysts further affected the perceived decline of religious orders in the later Middle Ages: the fiscalization of the papacy during the Avignonese captivity and the Schism,[46] the consolidation of state institutions and territorial dominions,[47] uprisings and feuds,[48] as well as biological forces such as plague and famine.[49] Popes and councils engaged in maneuvers to establish or enlarge their respective obediences.[50] An internal drive to reform the Church invigorated the foundational aspects of religious orders.[51] Several reform-minded popes and bishops in the early fifteenth century hailed from orders and communities like the Observance.[52] Their actions yielded short-term benefits to the orders through the bestowal and affirmation of privileges, along with a relaxation in religious practices.[53] However, severe consequences are well-documented, with instances where orders were so divided that general masters opposed one another, chapters clashed, and provinces and individual convents quarreled over recognizing a particular pope.[54]

Prior to the Western Schism (1378-1417), a parallel process of disintegration was already underway, driven by conflicts between imperial aspirations and the papal authority.[55] The Curia, the central governing body of the Church, augmented its influence and financial resources. This expansion targeted large abbeys and monastic foundations, which were large landholders during the late Middle Ages. Fiscal impositions in the form of increased taxation, autonomy constraints limiting the self-governance of religious orders, and economic interventions were not merely outcomes of internal ecclesiastical reforms or external pressures

---

46 Bowman (2014) discusses the fiscal challenges and administrative changes within the papacy during the Avignon Papacy and the ensuing Schism.
47 Nelson (1996).
48 Tuchman (1978) explores the social and political upheavals of the fourteenth century, including uprisings and feuds that affected religious communities.
49 Herlihy (1997) examines the impact of the Black Death and famine on European society, including the strain these biological forces placed on religious orders.
50 Baumgartner (2003) details the strategies employed by popes and councils to assert authority and manage obediences during periods of division and conflict.
51 Duffy (2006) analyzes the internal reform movements within the Church, emphasizing efforts to revitalize religious orders from within.
52 Madden (2010) focuses on the rise of reform-minded popes and bishops from reformed orders like the Observance, detailing their influence in the early fifteenth century.
53 Leech (2017) discusses the benefits and changes within religious orders resulting from the actions of reformers, including the bestowal of privileges and relaxed practices.
54 Ware (2009) provides case studies and accounts of the deep divisions and conflicts within religious orders during the Schism.
55 Izbicki (2009).

from secular authorities.[56] Instead, they represented modalities to consolidate and manage the Church's extensive temporal holdings more effectively. Concurrently, developing state structures in various European regions intersected with these ecclesiastical transformations. As emerging nation-states sought to centralize power, their administrative and fiscal policies impacted the Church's traditional privileges. The growing consolidation of urban economies and political power played a pivotal role in reshaping the landscape in which monastic congregations operated. Urban centers became hubs of economic negotiation and political maneuvering, contesting the Church's influence.[57] These interrelated forces operated in tandem to influence the internal organization of religious orders and monastic congregations. The push for administrative efficiency and financial solvency clashed with the orders' longstanding traditions and, consequently, many congregations found themselves in webs of obligations to which they were forced to answer.

In urban contexts, we find an added set of motivations for spiritual reform. Religious uncertainty resulting from the Black Death led to public acts of penance and apocalyptic preaching, with many seeking solace in the practices of asceticism.[58] Religious considerations played a role among urban circles interested in revitalizing their towns. Concerns about preserving religious life, advancing education and welfare, and addressing challenges posed by unregulated religious orders prompted urban authorities' support for reform initiatives.[59] When faced with the choice of backing or resisting the Observant movement, city councils saw an opportunity to exert influence over spiritual institutions.[60] In a broader context, the politics of religious life and the endorsement of reform, particularly the Observant movement, aligned with fifteenth-century trends that shifted power away from the church and contributed to the rise of a robust urban society.[61]

Despite the occasional impediments, the Observance reached a wide extent, moving beyond the borders of Italy and even of the Western Christendom. Bernardino Aquilano's chronicle shows that the Observants were experiencing numerical and spiritual growth in

---

56 Favier (1966).
57 Epstein (1993).
58 Lerner (1981).
59 Duggan (1978).
60 Delcorno (2023).
61 Delcorno (2023).

fifteenth-century Italy, spurring missionary fervor across vast territories.[62] Establishing posts not only in parts of Western and Central Europe but also in the Eastern Mediterranean, and Aegean islands revealed their ambitions, while the abandonment of some Observant communities due to Ottoman advances echoed strategies of pragmatic retreat.[63]

An important factor contributing to the spread of the Observance was thus the high mobility of its members, who traveled across far-away provinces. If in the late fourteenth century the emphasis was on contemplation and the recovery of eremitic traditions, with Bernardino of Siena and John Capistrano, the fifteenth-century Observance became popular in cities and among the lay urban population as convents were opened and preachers attracted large crowds of believers.[64] Reflecting this reality of growth and clash with local developments, Popes Eugene IV and Nicholas V entrusted John Capistrano with the task of fighting against the heresies in the regions beyond the Alps.[65] Over the course of many journeys, Capistrano preached in favor of solving conflicts between various factions of the nobility, a role commonly assigned to papal legates. However, Capistrano was not an official representative of the papacy but fulfilled an exceptional and similar role, as in his relation with Jan Rokyczana, the Hussite theologian, against whom he often spoke.[66] In his long career, he was only the most visible example of the Observants and a continuator of the institutional program of Bernardino of Siena of reforming the Franciscan order.

The Franciscan Observants were not unique in their pursuits of ideals of poverty and religious support. Ever since the thirteenth century, much like the Franciscans, the Dominican Observants engaged in the spiritual care of penitents and sought to weave a narrative around founding a Dominican 'third order'. Contemporary and medieval tales of Dominican history recount endeavors in the 1280s to forge a formal connection between penitents and Dominican friars. The conventional narrative asserts that Munio of Zamora, the Dominican Master General, wrote a rule in 1285 or 1286 placing penitents under friar supervision.[67] However, owing to the inherent tension between the Franciscan and Dominican orders, Pope Nicholas IV, a Franciscan himself, declined to endorse this

---

62 Romagnoli (2011).
63 Tolan (2002).
64 Zarri (2015).
65 Mixson (2016a) and Kalous & Stejskal (2020).
66 Pellegrini (2017).
67 Hujbers (2018), 101.

rule. Instead, he endeavored to consolidate penitents under the care of the Franciscans whom he thus placed in a better position.

I.2. The pillars of Observance

As noted, a feature that ensured the long-term stability and success of the Observance was that, ever since its early decades, the order relied on the active involvement of several personalities, referred to in the Observant writings as the four *pillars* of Observance (*quattuor columnae Observantiae*): Bernardino of Siena, John Capistrano, James of the Marches, and Albert Berdini of Sarteano. It was the first two of them who received an enhanced attention in the chronicles. Bernardino of Siena (1380-1444) played a special part in the history of the Observance. Having received a solid legal education, he left his small hermitic community and began preaching to the public. He traveled intensely as cities invited him to speak in public, where he received acclamations. Bernardino adopted a heavy moralizing position and preached against Jews, homosexuality, or usury.[68] Even if he was charged with accusations of heresy and had to defend himself in a trial organized in Rome, he founded convents which enhanced his reputation in the church at large. Two *vitae* and a longer account of his life in Bernardino Aquilano's *Chronicle* reflect his popularity.[69]

It was Bernardino who emphasized the idea of changing the Franciscan education system, though one can question to what extent this had been done in a systematic way. From 1424 to 1425, Bernardino preached in Florence, where he spoke publicly during a time of deep changes for the city.[70] In his sermons, he often voiced opinions not only on religious topics but on other aspects as well, like the spread of humanist ideas, pedagogy, or economic life. The focus on aspects of immediate practical concerns like morality and economics, helped Bernardino thus emerge as more popular than other preachers of his time, such as the Dominicans.[71]

Beyond his role as a model preacher, Bernardino of Siena was also a key figure in the institutional development of the Observant movement. He established Observant houses and promoted Observant reforms throughout Italy and beyond. He secured papal recognition and backing for the Observants by creating a distinct identity for the movement within the larger Franciscan order.[72] In this sense, Bernardino can be seen as

---

68   Muessig (2015).
69   Aquilano, *Chronicle*, 24-38.
70   Debby (2001).
71   Debby (2014).
72   Debby (2001).

not only a defender of the Observant family but also as one of its main creators, laying the groundwork for future growth and development. Aquilano's characterization of Bernardino as "maximus defensor, auctor et conservator nostrae familiae" reflected the Observants' debt to him as a mentor and guide.[73]

Alongside Bernardino of Siena, John Capistrano (1386-1456) was the other towering personality among the fifteenth-century Observants. A close associate of Bernardino whose manner of preaching he imitated,[74] Capistrano undertook a legal education in his youth while the political connections of his family prepared him for a leading position. Soon, however, following a personal revelation, he embraced the ideals of the Observance and began directing his efforts against the growing movements of Hussitism and Wycliffism and towards the unity of the church. In the last years of his life, he became critical of the humanist project of education and militated for a crusade against the Ottomans who had recently conquered Constantinople (1453) and threatened Western Europe. In the section dedicated to John Capistrano, Bernardino Aquilano's narrative emphasizes his role in the spread of Observance as well as his victory in the crusade against the Turks. Upon his death in 1456, Capistrano chose to be buried in Ilok, close to Belgrade, which suggests his attachment to the project of defending Central Europe from the growing Ottoman threat.[75] His legacy found reflection in hundreds of letters and sermons, while his biography was narrated in several popular *vitae*, like those of Nicolaus de Fara and Christopher Varese, as well as in historical narratives, like Michael of Carinthia's *Chronicle*.[76]

I.3. Medieval discourses of virtues and reform

With its emphasis on reform and spiritual renewal, the Observant movement responded not only to societal or political changes but was also rooted in the tradition and intellectual framework of medieval ethical thought. As the movement evolved and spread geographically, it both drew from, and contributed to ongoing reflections about key ethical notions like virtue, vice, and the nature of human morality. In many ways the Observants' focus on moral exemplarity and spiritual purity represented

---

73 See Aquilano, *Chronicle*, 6.20 and Delcorno (2015), 151.
74 Langer (2017).
75 Housley (2004).
76 Checcoli (2013).

a practical application of medieval virtue ethics. Therefore, to evaluate the Observant perspective emerging also through an engagement with contemporary moral philosophy and theology, a preliminary examination of the late medieval discourse on virtues and moral reform will provide an understanding of the context and motivations behind the movement's teachings and practices.

Foremost, medieval ethics discourse displayed affinities to ancient ethics, in particular Aristotelian notions of virtues.[77] This connection manifested especially in Thomas Aquinas' synthesis of Aristotelian virtue ethics with Christian theology, where he integrated the classical cardinal virtues (prudence, justice, fortitude, and temperance) with the Christian theological virtues (faith, hope, and charity). Other medieval thinkers like Peter Abelard expanded on ancient ethical frameworks by developing theories of intention and moral psychology, arguing that the moral worth of an action depends not merely on its external manifestation but on the agent's internal disposition and conscious choice. But the differences between ancient and medieval ethics were as important as the elements they shared. Fundamentally, unlike the classical thinkers who perceived virtue as the realization of an inherent human potential for goodness, medieval scholars saw it as a triumph over the inherent flaws that have plagued humanity since the Fall.[78] More than the doctrinal specifics, it was the beliefs and the pastoral practice that shaped medieval reflections on virtue.

Medieval thinking on virtue acknowledged the narrative of the fall of human nature. It emphasized that, within the Christian framework, virtue was a battleground where individuals confronted instincts and desires.[79] Due to the inherent fallen nature of humanity, virtue remained fragile, it could be easily compromised by sin, and its restoration demanded significant efforts. This stood in stark contrast to Aristotle's perspective, where virtues, once cultivated in youth, solidified into enduring habits that fostered inner equilibrium, allowing individuals to act in harmony with their moral convictions with ease. Even Thomas Aquinas highlighted the shortcomings in Aristotle's understanding of human nature by emphasizing the perpetual vulnerability of virtues to vice, with divine grace being the sole antidote.[80]

---

77 Nederman (1996).
78 Bejczy (2011), 223-283.
79 Bejczy (2011), 39-40.
80 Irwin (2005).

As scholars noted, the late medieval period witnessed a surge in the interest for defining virtues, which coincided with a scrutiny of human moral flaws.[81] The treatment of vices underwent transformations, varying according to the perspectives adopted by different authors in the fourteenth and fifteenth centuries. Already, centuries before, Gregory the Great streamlined the old monastic scheme of eight capital sins to seven, a framework of vices that became more prominent in medieval pastoral literature than any corresponding set of virtues. However, it is notable that the cardinal virtues were not always included in these treatises, despite the early acknowledgment of their capacity to resist sin. Instead, other virtues played a similar role in countering vices. This dynamic is exemplified in older works such as Prudentius' *Psychomachia* and Ambrosius Autpertus' widely circulated *De conflictu vitiorum et virtutum.* Both texts dramatized battles and disputes between the capital vices and various "contrary" or "remedial" virtues, notably by omitting the cardinal virtues from these portrayals.[82] This omission highlighted the evolving nature of the discourse on virtues and vices, as authors sought to understand the relationships among these moral concepts and to adapt them to the changing cultural and religious conditions of their time.

Such variations in moral thought and representation of virtues and vices originated in long-standing philosophical and theological tendencies from earlier centuries. We find notable instances where the cardinal virtues were depicted as the leaders of the group of virtues, the *turma virtutum*, that waged war against the vices. Earlier on, Bede, Alcuin, and other Carolingian authors emphasized this opposition between the four virtues and the eight capital vices.[83] While similar examples surface in the twelfth century, it remained uncommon for medieval moral writings to contrast the vices with the cardinal virtues. Even Alan of Lille's *De virtutibus et de vitiis*, which categorizes the moral qualities under the four cardinal virtues and the vices under the seven deadly sins, does not present the four virtues as the primary adversaries of the vices. Instead, the treatise concludes with an exploration of the gifts of the Holy Spirit, which, as seen in other twelfth-century writings, are portrayed as antidotes to capital vices.[84]

---

81 Bejczy (2011).
82 Bejczy (2011), 225.
83 Bejczy (2011), 226.
84 Wilks (1977).

It was only in the later periods that medieval moral literature opposed the capital vices to the cardinal virtues. Long before the Observants, Halitgar of Cambrai, dedicated the first book of his penitential text to the eight capital vices and their corresponding remedies, which encompassed contrary virtues and admonitions. He organized the second book around the seven virtues, indicating that he did not perceive the seven virtues as the primary adversaries of the vices. However, from the twelfth century onwards, there is a noticeable increase in texts and visual depictions that juxtapose the seven capital vices and their subcategories with the seven principal virtues, from which all other virtues emanate.[85] The trend finds a fitting illustration in the later works of Conrad of Hirsau, *De fructibus carnis et spiritus* and *Speculum virginum*. These compositions present a symmetrical pair of trees representing the vices and virtues, with pride (superbia) and humility (humilitas) at their respective roots. Each tree features seven main branches symbolizing the principal vices and virtues, while the twigs or leaves on each branch represent their corresponding subcategories.[86] It is worth noting that these tree depictions of virtues were more widely disseminated in the Middle Ages than previously recognized, and the accompanying definitions were transmitted independently of the visual representations.[87]

Catalogues of medieval virtues and vices also knew a wide distribution. Many examples showcasing such lists expand upon or challenge the traditional double heptad. One notable instance appears in the work of James of Benevent, a Dominican friar, whose widely circulated *Viridarium consolationis* includes twenty additional vices alongside the eight deadly sins, as well as twenty-seven supplementary virtues to complement the seven principal ones. Another work attributed to Pope Celestin V, titled *Opuscula de virtutibus et vitiis*, enumerates no less than sixty-two virtues in addition to the seven principal ones, the gifts, and the beatitudes, while also addressing thirty-one vices beyond the seven deadly sins. Moving forward in time, the late-thirteenth-century *Paradisus animae*, which focused on virtues, presents the theological and cardinal virtues amidst a collection of thirty-four other virtues. The *Liber Floretus*, a moral poem popular in schools during the fourteenth century, appends sections concerning the gifts, the beatitudes, and seventeen additional virtues to its treatment of the theological and cardinal virtues. Late medieval theological *florilegia*

---

85 Bateson (1894).
86 Bejczy (2011), 228.
87 Bajczy (2011), 242.

also blend the septenaries with other frameworks, including the gifts, the beatitudes (reduced to seven for numerical symmetry), the seven petitions of the Lord's Prayer, and the Ten Commandments. While condensed versions of such *florilegia* that deal with virtues and vices abound, even these moral collections incorporate supplementary schemes pointing to the versatility of the medieval system of virtues.[88]

I.4. Observant modulations of the medieval system of moral virtues

The continuous changes and adaptations occurring in the system of virtues of medieval thought offered a fertile ground for the Observants' construction of their moral stance. To be sure, if the Observants drew from this rich theoretical tradition, they applied previous concepts in ways that were fitting to their movement and its goals. Their approach featured a pragmatic and accessible interpretation of virtuous living, one that resonated with both the clergy and the laity. This shift in focus from abstract conceptualization to concrete practices marked a significant development in the late medieval spirituality of the Observant movement.

The practical orientation manifested itself in their choice and treatment of specific virtues. Poverty, obedience, and sometimes eremitism emerged as the virtues which the Observants favored. Yet, apart from their continuous mention, Observant authors planned a coherent system of virtues since this pursuit of virtues was a practical not a theoretical endeavor. Chroniclers explain virtues through miracles, like Glassberger when he discusses the virtue of obedience:

> Ex tunc nullum miraculum fecit. Nescio, quid potius in hac re mirandum, Francisci meritum, an obedientiae virtus, cuius vi se subiectos Sancti ostendunt in coelo.

> He performed no miracle from that time on. I do not know what is more admirable in this matter, the merit of Francis, or the virtue of obedience, by whose power the Saints show themselves obedient in heaven.[89]

In other cases, the emphasis on the practice of specific virtues becomes crucial in recruiting new friars, as Bernardino Aquilano suggests when he correlates it with the growth of the Order:

---

88 Bejczy (2011), 230.
89 Glassberger, *Chronicle*, 32. All translations in this book are mine, unless indicated otherwise.

> Postquam vero fratres numero et virtute creverunt, de sola Italia minime steteve contenti, sed fervore caritatis accensi ultra Italiam se extenderunt.

> But after the brothers increased in number and virtue, they were not content with only Italy, but, inflamed by fervor of charity, they spread beyond Italy.[90]

Yet, if the Observants' pursuit of practical virtue served as a tool for spiritual growth, it also thrust them into the ideological conflicts within the Franciscan Order. The very virtues they championed became battlegrounds for legitimacy and authority. This tension was evident in the realm of polemics, where virtues became both shields and weapons in the ongoing disputes between the Observants and Conventuals. Quick to critique the perceived moral laxity of the Conventuals, the Observants found themselves in a weaker position when it came to justifying their actions. The decision to separate from the authority of the Ministers General, the designated superiors of the Franciscan Order, required careful navigation of the moral principle of obedience. To counter the Conventuals' accusations of disobedience, the *Constitutiones Bernardini*, the most important fifteenth-century exposition of the Observant order issued in 1440, emphasized obedience while the *Bulla Concordiae* of 1456 included a vow of nearly unlimited obedience to the Conventual Minister General.[91] To that extent, Observant authors challenged the strict interpretation of obedience while maintaining it at the center of their moral commitments.

Gradually, the emphasis on virtues came to be associated with stricter observance as Observant authors became reluctant to accept other Franciscans adopting a lax interpretation of the Rule. In opposition to the Conventuals, they did not tolerate oscillations in the respect for the Rule. The delegate of the Conventuals at the Council of Basel, François Futz, identified six different ways of observing the Rule, ranging from relaxed conventualism to strict observance.[92] By accommodating all levels within his congregation, Futz prioritized preserving unity through flexibility, allowing various degrees of adherence within their ranks. Still, the Observants demanded a higher level of collective uniformity and, since the only

---

90   Aquilano, *Chronicle*, 15.
91   Lappin (2011).
92   Viallet (2016a), 79.

legitimate interpretation of the Rule was the Observant one, they reserved their harshest contempt for those who advocated a different path.[93]

If the Observants' insistence on strict adherence to the Rule and their emphasis on collective uniformity defined their approach to most virtues, their treatment of poverty, the virtue that stood at the heart of the Franciscan movement, demonstrated a nuanced approach. The Observants saw themselves as heirs to the original vision of Saint Francis, seeking to reclaim the order's charism of radical poverty and simplicity that had been eroded over time. This pursuit of evangelical poverty, which partly had to do with their concerns for the lay urban communities, shaped their identity, practices, and even their critiques of the broader Franciscan community.

The chronicles of Nicholas Glassberger and Bernardino Aquilano offer vivid portrayals of how poverty permeated all aspects of Observant life and thought. Glassberger extolled the virtues of poverty, and in numerous illustrations he highlighted it as "the brightest pearl in the crown of the Minor brothers."[94] He recounted, for instance, how early Observants embraced extreme austerity, living in dilapidated friaries and subsisting on alms begged door-to-door.

Bernardino Aquilano, on the other hand, documented the struggles and controversies surrounding poverty within the Franciscan Order.[95] He chronicled the heated debates between the Conventual and Observant factions, with the latter accusing the former of abandoning their vows of poverty through amassing wealth and property.[96] The Observants saw themselves as the true heirs to Franciscan poverty, while denouncing the Conventuals as having strayed from the order's founding principles.[97]

For the Observants, poverty was not an ascetic practice but a theological and spiritual commitment. They believed that embracing material poverty allowed them to imitate Christ more fully and to live out the radical Gospel message. They saw poverty as a means of purification, stripping away attachments to worldly possessions and liberating the soul for union with God.[98]

Within the Observant communities, this pursuit of poverty manifested in various ways. Friaries were constructed to be austere, devoid of ornate decorations or unnecessary comforts. The Observants rejected the

---

93 Mixson (2015).
94 Glassberger, *Chronicle*, 86.
95 Aquilano, *Chronicle*, 3.
96 Aquilano, *Chronicle*, 10.
97 Aquilano, *Chronicle*, 11 and 47-48.
98 Zarri (2015), 38.

accumulation of any superfluous possessions, often living in cramped and modest quarters. Their habits were made of coarse, inexpensive cloth, and they went barefoot or wore simple sandals. The chronicles reflect this reality as well.[99] Glassberger recounts how the Observants strictly adhered to the rule of begging for alms, relying entirely on the charity of the faithful for their sustenance.[100] This practice not only reinforced their vow of poverty but also fostered the bonds with the local communities they served. Aquilano, too, described how Observant friars would go on "questing" journeys, traveling from town to town to solicit donations of food, clothing, and other essentials.[101]

Furthermore, both chronicles deploy examples of the Observants' emphasis of spiritual poverty, a detachment from self-will, ambition, and the pursuit of honors or prestige. They believed that true poverty required humility, obedience, and a complete surrender to God's will. Such emphasis on poverty shaped the Observants' critiques of realities in the Franciscan Order and the Church at large. They decried wealth, property, and worldly power by religious orders and ecclesiastical institutions, viewing it as a betrayal of the Gospel ideals of simplicity and detachment. Aquilano's chronicle is replete with indictments of the Conventual Franciscans for their perceived laxity and embrace of comforts whereas in Glassberger's narrative multiple accounts shed a negative light on the Conventuals' customs.[102]

Still, variations from this stance towards the supreme value of poverty were not uncommon. It was Bernardino of Siena in the early fifteenth century who, even though he recognized the Franciscan vow of poverty, also understood that an excessive emphasis on this virtue could lead the Order into a destructive crisis. This negative attitude to material possessions had even resulted in the emergence of radical groups like the *Fraticelli*.[103] Consequently, he took measures to temper the emphasis on poverty within his community. The *Constitutiones Bernardini* of 1430, which recommended a moderate level of poverty in the Observance, were partially authored by Bernardino.[104] This restrained approach was also evident in his sermons, particularly in an address on poverty (c. 1439), in which Bernardino distanced himself from the notion that poverty was the

---

99 Silberer (2014), 281-285
100 E.g. Glassberger, *Chronicle*, 8.
101 Aquilano, *Chronicle*, 28-35.
102 E.g. Aquilano, *Chronicle*, 47 and Glassberger, *Chronicle*, 285.
103 Tsougkarakis (2018).
104 Lappin (2000), 34-40.

greatest virtue with eschatological importance. He argued that poverty was not a virtue in itself, but that true merit lay in indifference towards possessions. According to Bernardino, even wealthy individuals could be in possession of the virtue of poverty if only they regarded their material possessions to be worthless.[105] Nonetheless, Bernardino maintained the view that voluntary poverty was a virtuous act which reflected Christ's model. In the footsteps of other Franciscans, he connected poverty with acts of persecution, pointing out that Christ promised the kingdom of heaven only to those who were poor in spirit and those who showed patience in times of oppression.[106]

According to Bernardino, who echoed the Observant view about virtues, obedience was superior to poverty. Reflecting the same *Constitutiones Bernardini*, he exhorted the Observants to prioritize obedience as the key element of religion. Bernardino's emphasis on obedience was based on theological and philosophical arguments. He articulated a hierarchy, wherein the body is subjected to the mind, the mind to the soul, and ultimately, the soul to God. In support of this idea, he cited Saint Augustine's argument that "Obedience is the will of God" and argued that obedience reflected one's mastery of the mind leading to the control of the body, which, in turn, was the key to attaining comprehensive knowledge of God.[107]

Arranging virtues in hierarchies was popular among the Observants, as noted by Clare Lappin who showed that Observant authors dealt with the creation of an order of preeminence among virtues. Oddi authored the *Specchio de l'Ordine*, a book for a Franciscan Observant audience in which he gave an account of virtues with the intention to make it available to every Franciscan, regardless of the education level.[108] His work, written in the Tuscan-Umbrian dialect, had thirteen chapters, each dedicated to the treatment of a specific virtue and corresponding to Saint Francis' thirteen companions. Surprisingly, he did not single out poverty but preferred to praise the other Observants for their patience, a quality which he assigned to the martyrs. He also highlighted the virtue of charity which, he believed, was connected with the practice of preaching seen as a practical way of showing love in opposition to the contemplation of the Fraticelli. Even later, Mariano da Firenze, an author who believed that poverty was the supreme virtue, accepted that this virtue was rather a feature defining

---

105 Lappin (2000), 37-39.
106 Glassberger, *Chronicle*, 337.
107 Lappin (2000), 35.
108 Oddi, *La Franceschina*, ed. N. Cavna, 1929.

the communities in the past. His *Compendium Chronicarum* (1521) emphasized the idea of moderation, but added that only those "four pillars of Observance" could have practiced it.[109]

Glassberger's chronicle further illustrates the complex, even contradictory, meanings of Franciscan poverty. The account dedicated to Saint Francis' life includes an episode that turns poverty into an essential virtue but also subtly implies that poverty alone might not be enough to grow and sustain such a diverse movement. While Saint Francis was away on a mission, the vicars he left in charge, Philip and John, modified the Order's dietary rules, causing a lay brother to take his concerns directly to Saint Francis. News then reached Saint Francis that in his absence, the unity of the Order had fractured. Philip sought worldly power (legal authority), while John broke away in an attempt to establish his own group of followers. Frustrated by his lack of progress with the Saracens, Saint Francis returned to mend the Order and reemphasized the core Franciscan ideals: poverty, humility, and obedience.[110] This episode was more than a simple story from Saint Francis' life for it revealed the tension among the early Franciscans. Some members saw poverty as an end in itself, demanding simple living and a rejection of worldly power. Others understood the need for a more organized movement with better-trained friars to deal with the complex social and religious structures of the era. This latter view implies that education had a central role to play, though likely subordinate to the ideal of poverty.

Francis' reassertion of the primacy of poverty and humility over ambition and self-promotion appears as an attempt to safeguard the Order's identity and prevent further fracturing. Poverty becomes a unifying force for other virtues, meant to curb individual agendas and make sure the Franciscan movement remains focused on its original ideals. However, Glassberger's chronicle does not offer a simple condemnation of education or worldly engagement. He suggests that the actions of the two friars, Philip and John, however misguided, could have stemmed from the recognition that a large and influential movement cannot function solely on radical poverty. Other episodes in Glassberger's account of Saint Francis' life confirm the tendency to nuance poverty and also point to the importance of providing guidance and education to the growing Franciscan community.[111] A telling example was Francis' decision to appoint Brother

---

109   Lappin (2000), 178-216.
110   Glassberger, *Chronicle*, 17.
111   Glassberger, *Chronicle*, 36.

Elias as his successor, despite the fact that Elias' reputation for worldly wisdom may have contributed to the eventual divisions within the order and the rise of the Observant movement.[112]

These episodes signal a widespread interest in reform, reflecting the points of tension between ideals and practicalities that characterized the Franciscan Observant movement. The emphasis on a life of poverty and preaching the Gospel was a response to the perceived need for renewal within the Church.[113] However, as we have already seen throughout the above analysis and as it will become clearer in the following sections, the chronicles under analysis here show that the implementation of these ideals was not straightforward. It required further modulation and harmonization with other local realities or discourses particularly with regard to political changes and education. In the following, I will turn to a discussion of these areas.

I.5. The Observants and the medieval discourses of power

On many occasions, the Observants engaged in regional politics, though the narrow focus on religious reform obscured their political discourse. This political engagement, however, was not about advancing a fixed political doctrine, but rather applying a distinctly Franciscan understanding of social bonds and obligations to the political sphere. Like their theological predecessors, Observants viewed societal relationships as rooted in promises and mutual responsibilities, offering a framework for navigating political complexities and promoting peace. This framework allowed them to maintain credibility as spiritual reformers and to participate in political mediation, since their self-imposed distance from formal power structures enhanced their authority as neutral arbiters.[114] Bernardino of Siena's arrival in Siena in August 1427, shortly after declining the pope's invitation to become the city's bishop, illustrates this dynamic.[115] His refusal to undertake a position of power reinforced his reputation as a man of God, a favorite of the people, enabling him to act as a trusted peacemaker during a time of political unrest. Government officials, recognizing his ascetic credibility and persuasive preaching, invited him to deliver a seven-week cycle of sermons aimed at diffusing

---

112   Glassbergr, *Chronicle*, 32.
113   Glassberger, *Chronicle*, 13 and 17.
114   Lambertini (2005), 151-157.
115   Muessig (2015), 190.

tensions among urban factions. This approach was characteristic of the Observants' engagement in public matters during the first half of the fifteenth century, as their involvement in political and ecclesiastical issues deepened. While Bernardino's sermons focused on transforming individuals into better Christians and not on advocating for radical political change, such efforts reflected the entanglement of religious reform and political discourses of the late Middle Ages.

Their interaction with secular power differed from the approach to papal power, which was grounded in canon law and papal decretals.[116] The Observants' political reform agenda was influenced by several factors: their relationship with authority, the desire for church unity, and the crusades against the Ottomans.[117] Numerous Observant friars served as papal legates and advisors to kings, mediating conflicts between secular rulers and the Church, their reputation for austerity and moral authority making them valuable intermediaries in late medieval politics.[118] The Observants also used their preaching skills to shape public opinion on political matters, particularly in Italian city-states, addressing issues of governance, justice, and social reform in their sermons.[119] Furthermore, Observant Franciscans took part in ongoing exchanges concerning church governance, with some backing conciliar theory and others defending papal supremacy, reflecting the Order's engagement with ecclesiastical politics.[120]

Like with the conceptualization of virtues, the Observants adapted their approach to governance and the discourses of power. The fourteenth and fifteenth centuries were formative periods for the development of new ideas of power and political reform. Fundamental principles of late medieval political thinking continued to rely on Aristotle and, increasingly, on Augustine: both were interpreted in a novel way to justify the autonomy of the political order, but by means of religious doctrine rather than of political philosophy.[121]

The political thought of this era centered on the origins of legitimate power and the challenge of unified governance. Thinkers like Marsilius of Padua, John of Paris, and William of Ockham addressed this issue through

---

116 Moorman, 1968.
117 Housley, 1992.
118 Musco, 2013.
119 Debby, 2014.
120 Izbicki, 2008b.
121 Izbicki, 2008a.

the lens of the relationship between spiritual and temporal power.[122] Many sought to determine whether a monarch's authority derived from God, the people, or from both. The debates revolved around the respective roles and jurisdictions of the papacy versus secular rulers, kings, emperors, or local leaders. Thinkers examined concepts like sovereignty, consent, and natural law in attempting to establish foundations for legitimate political authority. Bartolus and Baldus argued that entities not recognizing a superior (like independent cities or kings) achieved *de facto* the same powers within their territories as the emperor enjoyed *de iure* in the empire. This led to concepts like "civitas sibi princeps" (the city is its own prince) and "rex in regno suo est imperator regni sui" (the king in his kingdom is the emperor of his kingdom).[123] John of Paris, for his part, argued that while God was the ultimate source of royal power, the selection of a king lay with the people whereas Marsilius of Padua emphasized the role of the "human legislator" (the people or corporate body of citizens) in instituting political authority. The tensions between universalist claims of papal and imperial power versus the emerging autonomy of kingdoms and city-states further complicated these reflections on the sources and nature of rightful rule. Along these lines, Nicholas of Cusa argued that legitimate power was derived from both God and the people, with naturally free people freely submitting to authority.[124] More drastically, Marsilius of Padua in his *Defensor Pacis* advocated for the separation of spiritual and temporal powers, proposing that political authority should be derived from the people.[125]

The Observants attended to these trends and reflected on the current political realities in their own way and with their own discursive instruments. Their texts conveyed critical messages against political decisions, advocated courses of action like the Crusades, while stressing their allegiance to the Pope. To that extent, the Observants tried to reclaim the ethical and the political domains through religious reform by transcending the constraints imposed by localized political authorities. According to Letizia Pellegrini, what truly distinguished the increasingly prevalent and influential preaching styles of fifteenth-century Observant orders was not merely their method of preaching or emotional impact on audiences, but their innovative ways of engaging

---

122   See Nederman (1995), Kilcullen (1993) and Coleman (1991).
123   Canning (2011).
124   Canning (2011).
125   Condren (1977).

with political authorities experimenting with non-traditional forms of governance.[126] Accordingly, the relationship between the discourse of spiritual reform and politics became one of mutual reinforcement. Preaching and disseminating ideas in written form justified power since it still depended on political circumstances, while also seeking to define moral conduct. Yet, in certain situations the preachers who began making direct and independent political claims, such as, famously, Savonarola, faced rejection. The latter's attempt to go beyond his role as a mediator between religious authorities and secular rulers by challenging political figures, resulted in a serious backlash.[127]

The preaching practices in Italy and beyond thus suggest that the Observants' primary concern of spiritual renewal became correlated to their discourse of general social reform and to the political ideals cultivated outside the Church. Parallel reform movements that sought to align both religious and secular authorities with divine law and moral order evidenced this intersection of spiritual renewal and political ideals. In 1438, an anonymous treatise titled *Reformatio Sigismundi* called for Emperor Sigismund and his nobles to work towards reforming the church and the world. The treatise focused on the religious orders, arguing that monks and canons had become too powerful, living in large communities with incorporated parishes and endowments. It criticized their arrogant behavior, such as riding horses, gambling, and buying or selling property and offices. The treatise denounced friars for begging and hearing confessions without proper authorization while identifying the root cause of this decline as a lack of obedience and observance within the religious orders. The author of the *Reformatio Sigismundi* posited a restoration of justice, peace, and the common good for Christendom by reverting to the ancient laws of the Empire and the Church, considered the tangible embodiment of divine law. Urging princes and prelates to codify and disseminate their ordinances among the population, he envisioned the ideal reformative leader as a knowledgeable priest-king versed in the law. Concrete proposals, such as detailed regulations for the attire of priests, doctors, and lawyers, as well as guidelines for fair wages and prices to protect the less privileged, were presented to reinstate a proper moral and social order.[128]

---

126 Pellegrini (2011).
127 Weinstein (1958).
128 Mixson (2015b), 63

Similarly, contemporaries conceptualized their visions of reform as a return to the social and moral order ingrained in laws, such as the "law of Christ" articulated by groups like the Lollards, referring to Scripture and purified, authentic practices. A pervasive culture of law permeated the society, whether in high-level politics or the ordinary life.[129] Lawyers, leveraging their expertise, became indispensable in the struggle, utilizing a plethora of decrees, precedents, and customs in their consultations (consilia), the opinions of which were increasingly documented and circulated.[130] Preachers and theologians blurred the lines between the legal, moral, and spiritual realms in their sermons and treatises. The convergence of the legal, moral, and social spheres found additional demonstration through the enactment of laws in urban centers, where rulers and councils anchored the various social classes, including the nobility, farmers, and clergy, to customary lifestyles amidst changing trends in consumption and presentation.[131] The Observants' evolving political discourse contributed to debates on legitimate authority, the administration of local communities, and church governance.[132] Through their preaching and reform efforts, they legitimized the attempts to align religious and secular authorities with divine law and moral order, demonstrating the inseparability of spiritual renewal and political ideals.

---

129 Viallet (2013) and Hudson (1988).
130 Brundage (2008).
131 More (2015).
132 Mixson (2009).

II

The Observant Discourse of Reform: Legitimation, Education, and Communication

So far, we have seen that the Observant discourse of reform emerged against the background of a substantial body of medieval moral ideas, a changing political landscape and growing appeals for a recommitment to spiritual ideals and the tenets of law. Clerics found themselves entrenched within dominant paradigms shaping both the ecclesiastical and societal landscapes for centuries. For its part, the Church found itself entangled in challenges, mirroring the relation between reform, legal practices, and political debates on the nature of authority. One persistent issue was that the individuals who withdrew from worldly pursuits, pledging allegiance to spiritual ideals, were far from their commitments. Paradoxically, those expected to provide spiritual models appeared in greater need of conversion and order than ever before.

To overcome these difficulties, the discourse of Observant reform adjusted to include not only appeals to action but also other elements like narratives, literary or political themes, and even particular figures of speech which became encoded into texts deriving from the Observant tradition. Topics like consultations with other religious groups and power brokers or accounts of episodes like the pursuit of heretics created a context for deploying Observant ideas of reform and became a central part of this discourse. Other non-political fields like education and even public health were deployed to generate meaningful images of a reformed religious life.

Essential for the Observant discourse of reform was the idea of the order's steady and substantial growth. The Observant chroniclers underscored that growth occurred as a vigorous response to a prolonged period of moral decline. In the debut of his chronicle, Glassberger emphasizes the role of Saint Francis and the Franciscan Order as reformers of the Church and society. He emphasizes the idea that Francis was part of God's plan of sending reformers, such as Noah, Abraham, Moses, and the prophets, at a moment when humanity has strayed from the path of righteousness. Following the Franciscan perspective, Glassberger portrays Saint Francis as the latest in this line of reformers, sent to renew the life of Christ and *the memory of His passion in the hearts of the faithful*.[133] Observant chronicles also described in detail the order's geographical expansion. For instance, Glassberger made great strides to show the early attempts of the Franciscan Order to expand beyond Italy, specifically when narrating the mission into the German lands (Teutonia). This gradual transfer beyond the Alps highlighted the Order's plan to spread its message and way of life to other parts of Europe, even in the face of challenges and setbacks.[134]

By following the order's growth in various geographical areas, we can also trace the goals of the Observant reform. Scholars argued that the main objective of the Observant preachers, especially those in John Capistrano's circle was to correct the imbalances and errors in religious practice.[135] Yet, this was not the only goal, since the chronicles point to a diversity of forms of religious life: regular or irregular, accepting or eluding canonical authority, innovative or returning to old ideals. Each of these forms necessitated a distinct approach and response from the Observant reformers. The chronicles show that the Observants had to adapt their strategies to address the specific challenges posed by each form of religious expression, balancing the need for correction with sensitivity to local traditions and practices.

Another hallmark of the Observant reform movement was the considerable effort to extend religious renewal beyond convents to lay communities.[136] This suggests the intention to revitalize religious life not only among Franciscan friars but also within the lay communities. To this end, the Observants who traveled far away from their residences, developed structured programs of religious instruction for devout

---

133 Glassberger, *Chronicle*, 26.
134 Glassberger, *Chronicle*, 11.
135 Viallet (2013).
136 Muessig (2015) and Roest (2000), 159.

laypeople, integrating them into their order's spiritual sphere.[137] While these individuals remained legally classified as laity under canon law, they adopted monastic practices in their daily lives. To formalize this new religious status, the Observants worked to secure legal recognition for these lay groups as legitimate ecclesiastical bodies.[138]

The Observant Franciscans' efforts to integrate devout laypersons into their spiritual sphere extended well beyond selected groups of penitents. They cultivated connections with groups of urban artisans and merchants, seeking to instill Franciscan values and practices within these influential segments of late medieval society. Through systematic religious instruction and creation of tertiary Franciscan orders, the Observants aimed at transforming the devotional lives of the laity. This allowed them to exert influence over the ethical conduct of the urban populace, as these lay followers adopted vows of poverty, chastity, and obedience, that mirrored the Observant friars.[139] They also recognized the value of co-opting the rising urban elites, whose social and economic power could bolster the Franciscan reform movement.[140]

Given their aim to guide both monastic circles and lay communities, their interest in the power of the written word to legitimize their outreach efforts increased.[141] Prolific Franciscan authors produced a wealth of devotional and instructional texts, which they disseminated through an ever expanding network. These works not only provided guidance to lay audiences on proper religious practice but also shaped a historical narrative that positioned the Observants as the rightful inheritors of the Franciscan legacy. By framing their reforms as a return to the original vision of Francis, the Observants, among other things, undermined the authority of other competing groups like the Conventual Franciscans and secured widespread acceptance for their initiatives. This discursive strategy enabled the Observants to present their activities as sanctioned by ecclesiastical tradition, further legitimizing their integration of the laity into the Franciscan fold.

In their approach to popular religious practice, the Observants promoted readily accessible models of devotion and spirituality. This is particularly evident in Bernardino Aquilano's chronicle of events in L'Aquila, which centers on Bernardino of Siena's career and death. Aquilano documented

---

137 Roest (2000), 304.
138 Delcorno (2015) and Mixson (2015b), 82.
139 Roest (2000), 306.
140 More (2015).
141 Delcorno (2015).

how Bernardino's reputation as a miracle worker sparked public demands for his canonization, arguing that these miracles both manifested divine power through the saint's intercession and strengthened popular faith.[142] His account served a dual purpose: demonstrating the saint's spiritual credentials while supporting the rigorous episcopal investigations required for canonization. A different emphasis appears in Glassberger's chronicle, which was also recording miracle-driven canonization efforts but focused more intensely on the supernatural aspects of these events.[143] Unlike Aquilano's emphasis on institutional validation, Glassberger highlighted individual mystical experiences, as exemplified in his detailed accounts of Franciscan missionaries' visions in Prussia.[144]

The discourse of reform merged ideas of model Observant virtues and practicalities of expansion in other areas of Europe beyond the Alps. Again, the chronicles offer illustrative examples. Glassberger deals with the process of introducing the Franciscan Observance reform movement into different provinces like in the case of the Province of Strasbourg in 1426.[145] In this episode, the chronicle recounts an episode involving Louis III, the Count Palatine of the Rhine, and his wife Mechtilde of Savoy, portrayed as a devout woman. They noticed that the Conventual Franciscans in Heidelberg were living in a way that was not in accordance with the Franciscan Rule. Mechtilde, who was familiar with the Observant Franciscans in her homeland of Savoy, urged her husband to invite Observant friars from the Province of Touraine to reform the Heidelberg friary. The Provincial Minister, Jodocus, was reluctant to allow friars from another province to take over the Heidelberg friary, fearing that it would be removed from his jurisdiction. He suggested that he could send friars from his own province, particularly from the friary in Rufach, to reform Heidelberg. As Glassberger remarks, the frequent transfer of friars by the Provincial Minister was considered an obstacle to the progress of the reform. The narrative then introduces Nicholas Caroli, a former priest who had joined the Franciscans and had been appointed Guardian of Heidelberg by the Provincial Minister. When the Observants decided to return to their province due to the frequent changes, Nicholas prepared to leave as well. However, Mechtilde persuaded him to stay, promising to bring more Observant friars who could not be easily

---

142   Aquilano, *Chronicle*, 35-36.
143   Glassberger, *Chronicle*, 302-303.
144   Glassberger, *Chronicle*, 286.
145   Glassberger, *Chronicle*, 283-285.

removed by the Provincial Minister. According to Glassberger, Mechtilde pleaded with her husband to send more Observant friars from Touraine. Initially, Louis was reluctant, as he was preoccupied with the Bohemian threat to his territories and planning a military expedition with the king. However, moved by his wife's tears and the pleas of the nobles present, he agreed and sent letters to the Vicar of the Province of Touraine requesting friars for the Heidelberg friary, promising to provide for their needs. In a fortunate turn of events, the Vicar sent devout and experienced friars who set a proper example, attracting students from the university to join the Order. Ending with the spread of the reform movement to other friaries, such as Pforzheim and Tübingen, under the patronage of other princes, the story thus exemplifies how the Observant reform discourse wove together essential elements: the moral imperative for religious renewal, the practical challenges of institutional expansion, the role of noble patronage, and even the tensions between local and trans-regional networks. This narrative, which Observant chronicles like Glassberger's plausibly borrowed from previous sources, demonstrates how reform initiatives required not only spiritual conviction but also careful navigation of political relationships, jurisdictional tensions, and geographic boundaries to establish model communities beyond the Alps. In doing so, it reinforced the representation of how the implementation of the Observance mirrored its ideological framework, where establishing exemplary religious communities served both as a demonstration of Observant virtues and as a blueprint for further expansion.

II.1. The Observants and their efforts at institutional legitimation

Another area in which the discourse of Observant reform developed was the order's relationship with the institutions of authority, whether the Church or other political leaders. Given the breadth of their narratives, both chronicles heavily illustrate this strategy. In the section dedicated to the Council of Constance in 1415, Glassberger recounts how the Observants obtained privileges and papal decrees.[146] The chronicle reproduces the document titled *Provisio Fratrum Minorum de Observantia* issued during the nineteenth session of the Council which discusses the relations between the Franciscan Observants and the Church, as well as the context of the Council's dealings with heresy and reform.

---

146 Glassberger, *Chronicle*, 252.

Furthermore, to stress the significance of the document, Glassberger provides an unusual amount of information on the ceremonial stages that led to adopting the legal document confirming the order. The session began with a Mass celebrated by Nicholas, Bishop of Assisi, followed by the singing of litanies and the reading of the Gospel. Cardinal Peter of Cambrai, one deputy in matters of faith, then announced that Jerome of Prague, who had been accused of heresy and imprisoned, wished to revoke his errors and return to the unity of the Christian faith. Jerome ascended the pulpit and denounced the heresies of John Wycliffe and Jan Hus, thereby submitting himself to the Church.[147]

Thereafter, Glassberger shifts focus to the Franciscan Observants. Four bishops, representing the Italian, French, German, and English nations, along with Berthold of Wildingen, an auditor of the Apostolic Palace, ascended the pulpit. Berthold read an ordinance, prepared by Cardinals Giordano Orsini and Peter of Cambrai, along with other deputies of the Council. This ordinance had been agreed upon by John of Rocha (Vicar General of the Conventuals) and other masters and members of the Conventual Franciscans on one side, and the Observants of the Provinces of France, Burgundy, and Touraine on the other. The ordinance which addressed the Observance of the Franciscan Rule by the Friars Minor reflected the growing prominence of the Franciscan Observant movement and the Church's attempts to navigate the tensions between Observants and Conventuals. By providing for the Observants' way of life and recognizing their distinct identity, Glassberger emphasized the idea that the Council of Constance promoted unity, reform, and orthodoxy within the Franciscan Order and the Church.[148]

In the same context of the order's relations with the authorities, Glassberger highlights the secular rulers who supported the legal sanctioning of the Observance. For instance, he deals with Sigismund, known for his involvement in the Council of Constance and his efforts for the unity of the Church. In an episode from 1410, he narrates how after the death of Rupert, King of the Romans, and during Wenceslaus' reign as King of Bohemia, the electors met in Frankfurt to choose a new king. They split into two groups: one supporting Jodocus, Margrave of Moravia, and the other backing Sigismund, King of Hungary. After a year-long indecision and Jodocus' death, the electors agreed on Sigismund, widely perceived as

---

147 Glassberger, *Chronicle*, 178-181.
148 Glassberger, *Chronicle*, 258-260.

a devout Christian known for his victories against the Turks and support for the Franciscans.[149]

To further emphasize the order's legitimacy, Glassberger pays much attention to events occurring during Sigismund's rule. In 1413, Ladislaus, the King of Sicily, captured Rome, at a time when Pope John XXIII and the Curia were in Florence. The Romans suffered plundering and many were taken to Naples. The Pope then sent messengers to Sigismund, King of the Romans, to decide on a location and time for a council. They chose Constance, a decision later confirmed by Pope John, who summoned all prelates to attend.[150]

Glassberger's accounts of the political personalities of his time provide multiple historical details about rulers or states. These references offer a precise picture of the events or characters involved. For instance, he depicts the complete sequence of events leading to the violence against the Franciscans in Prague:

> Anno Domini 1419 obiit dominus Wenceslaus, rex Bohemiae et olim etiam Romanorum, filius Caroli IV. imperatoris et frater Sigismundi, regis Hungariae et Romanorum; et coeperunt haeretici Hussitae Pragae ecclesias evertere, et seditionem facientes, lamentabiliter imagines Christi et Sanctorum sacrilego ausu combusserunt et destruxerunt. Conventum autem Fratrum Minorum apud sanctum Iacobum Pragae defenderunt carnifices adhuc catholici, fraternitatem suam ibi habentes. Celeri autem Religiosi ubique in eadem civitate magnam violentiam et depraedationem omnium bonorum et rerum suarum passi sunt ab haereticis et vetulis.
>
> In the year 1419, Lord Wenceslaus, the King of Bohemia and formerly also of the Romans, son of Emperor Charles IV and brother of Sigismund, the King of Hungary and of the Romans, died. Heretical Hussites in Prague began to destroy churches and, causing sedition, burned and destroyed images of Christ and the Saints with audacity. The convent of the Friars Minor at Saint James in Prague was defended by still-Catholic executioners, who maintained their brotherhood there. Meanwhile, the religious everywhere in the same city suffered great violence and plunder of all their goods and possessions from the heretics and rebels.[151]

---

149 Glassberger, *Chronicle*, 240.
150 Glassberger, *Chronicle*, 245.
151 Glassberger, *Chronicle*, 275.

However frequent, the references to legitimate ecclesiastical and lay authorities should not deceive us, as the Observant discourse of reform moved beyond historical concrete details and made appeals to emotions. A letter reproduced in the same chronicle by Glassberger and debating the Pope's legitimacy, makes large-scale use of emotionally charged language, to emphasize accusations against what was perceived as "wicked deeds.[152]" Such a language designed to stir up strong negative emotions in the reader, like anger and moral outrage, was also aimed at reinforcing the sense of urgency and the need for action. By framing the schism as a dramatic battle between good and evil, the author appeals to the readers' emotions and sense of moral righteousness, encouraging them to take a stand against the divisions within the Church.

Alongside the negative emotions, the discourse of reform employed the rhetoric of hope and promise, emphasizing the possibility of renewal and restoring true faith. The prologue of Glassberger's chronicle states the author's intention to provide "encouragement for religious fervor" to future generations.[153] Both Glassberger and Aquilano, while depicting the challenges to adhering to the rule, conflicts, and scandals, also suggest that a solution to the conflicts and moral decline can be found.[154] This optimistic language served to mobilize the audience, suggesting that through their collective efforts, the Church could overcome its ongoing turmoils and return to its righteous path. By balancing condemnation with encouragement, such a rhetoric of hope did not only galvanize opposition but underpinned the vision of a unified future. These examples show that the Observants' discourse of reform was not solely focused on critique and condemnation, but incorporated a positive message of solving tensions. This dual approach allowed them to both address the problems within the Church and inspire action towards a future of reform.

II.2. Integrating education in the Observant discourse of reform

In parallel to cultivating ecclesiastical and secular authority, the movement's engagement with education represented another level in the formation of their reformist identity.[155] Although, as with political thought where no precise doctrine was contoured, the Observants did not develop

---

152 Glassberger, *Chronicle*, 229-231.
153 Glassberger, *Chronicle*, 2.
154 E.g. Glassberger, *Chronicle*, 346.
155 On education in Observant circles see Delcorno (2015), Roest (2014), or Şenocak (2011).

a coherent pedagogical philosophy; instead, they created a distinctive educational framework that served both religious formation and lay instruction. This was built upon medieval educational foundations while it also innovated to meet their reform objectives. The present section will examine the movement's educational strategies at three levels: first, the relation between traditional learning and new contents and methodologies; second, the implementation of targeted pastoral instruction; and third, the Observants' navigation of competing demands between spiritual formation and circulation of knowledge. Special attention will be given to how influential figures like Bernardino of Siena and John Capistrano shaped Observant pedagogy in their rejection or integration of humanist learning and their use of chronicles as educational tools.

The assumption here is that the Observant educational project operated at the intersection of monastic tradition and pedagogical innovation, encompassing both religious formation and secular learning. While targeting specific audiences, from political elites to youth, parents, and clergy, the movement transcended simple moral instruction through preaching.[156] The Observants' educational framework incorporated the occasional study of classical authors and contemporary learning methods, adapting their approach to diverse regional contexts and pastoral needs. This vision contributed to the changes in late medieval educational practices while intensifying their reach across social categories and regional contexts.[157]

II.2.1. Late medieval ideas of education

As the reforms of the Church and society were organized around a system of discursive themes pertaining to preserving appropriate virtues and hierarchies, the Observants recognized the role that education played in shaping the minds and souls of both religious and lay people. Reformers could draw from a variety of sources and formulate an agenda whose terms and principles defined subsequent educational innovations. Drawing on the tradition of medieval pedagogy with its emphasis on dialogue, affects, and experience in the learning process, the Observants developed alternative approaches to instruction, and spiritual formation that were tailored to the needs of their audiences. Continuity and change as well as educational practices adjusted to various social groups (political authorities, clergy,

---

156   Mixson (2015), 148.
157   Mixson (2015), 149.

youth, or parents) were combined in the education system.[158] Even if moral instruction was at the heart of Observant reform, education included more than preaching.[159] Both Aquilano's and Glassberger's chronicles highlighted the order's increasing engagement with university education and scholastic theology. Several accounts depicted Francis sending Anthony of Padua to complete his theological studies. Other Franciscan theologians like Alexander of Hales, John of Parma, and Bonaventure who lectured at Paris received occasional mentions that echoed the order's intellectual tradition. The chronicles thus reflect a literate culture among the friars even though it contrasted the authors' focus on those who upheld a strict observance.

Sources confirm the premium value of education among the Franciscans. The fact that Saint Francis himself was able to preach effectively before the Pope and the College of Cardinals suggests that he possessed a high level of theological knowledge and rhetorical skill, which he acquired through informal education within the Order. A passage included in the account of the early years of the Franciscan history demonstrates that the connections between Franciscans and the Papacy went far and wide also geographically, up to the Holy Lands:

> Per idem tempus quidam e fratribus hoc ipsum domino Hugolino, Cardinali Episcopo Hostiensi, qui, defuncto domino Iohanne de sancto Paulo, Cardinali Episcopo Sabinensi, supradicti Ordinis protectore, se beato Francisco et fratribus in protectorem et procuratorem ex devotione obtulit, notificaverunt. Qui eos vexationibus praedictis redimere volens, vocatum ad se beatum Franciscum domino Papae Honorio praesentavit, quem reperit in negotiis Ordinis pium, favorabilem et benevolentem. Praedicante autem sancto Patre coram ipso Summo Pontifice et sacro senatu et Ordinem commendante, Spiritus Dei, qui in co loquebatur, tanta corda virorum illorum sublimium devotione ad Ordinem succendit, ut singuli ex fratribus aliquos ad secum morandum habere vellent. Petivit tunc etiam sanctus Franciscus a domino Papa praedictum dominum Hosliensem, de quo per visionem monitus fuit, et obtinuit in protectorem, qui primus hoc officium secundum formam regulae postulatus gessit. Eodem anno 1217 quidam monachus, Dithmarus nomine, perrexit ad Terram Sanctam, transiens sortes Zabulon et Nephtalim, venitque Semphoram oppidum, de quo sancta Anna, mater beatae Virginis, orta

---

158   Mixson (2015), 148.
159   Mixson (2015), 145.

est; similiter Nazareth civitatem pertransiit, et ipse scripsit librum de Terra Sancta et denuntiavit domino Papae statum eiusdem Terrae, qui, scilicet Papa Honorius, praedicavit Ierosolymitanum iter in civitate Roma, quod Innocentius inchoaverat.

In the same period, certain brothers presented themselves to Lord Hugolino, Cardinal Bishop of Ostia, who, after the passing of Lord John of Saint Paul, Cardinal Bishop of Sabina and protector of the aforementioned Order, offered themselves to Blessed Francis and the brothers as their protector and procurator out of devotion. Desiring to redeem them from the aforementioned vexations, he presented Blessed Francis to Pope Honorius, whom he found to be pious, favorable, and benevolent in the affairs of the Order. While Saint Francis was preaching before the Supreme Pontiff and the sacred senate, the Spirit of God, who was speaking through him, kindled such devotion in the hearts of those noble men toward the Order that each of the brothers desired to have some stay with him. At that time, Saint Francis also requested from the aforementioned Lord of Ostia, about whom he had been warned through a vision, and obtained him as the protector. He was the first to hold this office according to the rule's requirements. In the same year, 1217, a certain monk named Dithmarus journeyed to the Holy Land, passing through the territories of Zebulun and Naphtali. He arrived at the town of Semphora, where Saint Anne, the mother of the Blessed Virgin, was born. Similarly, he passed through the city of Nazareth and wrote a book about the Holy Land. He reported the state of the same land to the Pope, namely Pope Honorius, who preached the Jerusalem pilgrimage in the city of Rome, a journey that Innocent had initiated.[160]

Central to this educational effort that combined church authority, spiritual traditions, and secular life, was the concept of adaptation, which allowed the Observants to adjust their teaching methods and materials to suit the dynamic socio-political landscape of the time.[161] Occasionally, the adaptation involved the elimination of certain topics. For example, the Spanish Observants in Villacrecia developed a structured program of studies that excluded the liberal arts, as they believed these to be detrimental to the Franciscan order. Friars preparing for pastoral work received training primarily in applied theology. They studied Scripture interpretation

---

160   Glassberger, *Chronicle*, 12-13.
161   On adaptation as a literary process in general see Sanders (2015), 1-17.

using Nicolas of Lyra's commentaries, which dealt with literal and moral meanings. Their education included practical materials like confession guides, basic theological texts, moral theology summaries, sacramental administration manuals, and resources for sermon preparation and delivery.[162] By employing adaptive practices in rhetoric, dialectics, and other areas of learning, and by promoting preachers who could communicate effectively with different groups, the Observants hoped to create a more flexible and responsive educational system that could better serve the needs of the Church and society. Observant preachers stressed the importance of adapting their messages to suit their audience, and the order's renewed interest in learning,[163] which was not burdened by scholastic distinctions, suggests that the fifteenth-century Observant Franciscans and contemporary humanists shared similar views on the curriculum of studies.[164] The commitment to adaptation is clear in the wide range of texts produced by the Observants, from chronicles and hagiographies to preaching manuals and devotional works, which bear witness to the order's ongoing efforts to engage with the world around them. These texts were used in training Observant preachers, who relied on model sermons rather than the rules of the *Ars Praedicandi*.[165]

To better understand the practices of adaptation for pedagogical purposes, it is necessary to examine the role and development of late medieval educational practices, as different pedagogical approaches impacted students' intellectual growth to different degrees. Medieval education encompassed several tenets and widespread practices such as the use of specific genres like dialogue as a medium of education and philosophy, the role of emotions in both enabling and hindering learning, or the need for pedagogical readings in the late Middle Ages.[166] Medieval educators recognized the importance of adapting classical genres, such as annotated lists of proverbs, to serve new purposes. For example, oftentimes this minor classical genre was adapted to create a reference book that helped readers better understand their texts and the writers they were studying.[167] Educators encouraged their students to study popular orations, to observe how the authors adapted to a given situation, and to reflect on the situations and subject matters of their own writing. They regarded

---

162 Urribe & Jarffla (1958), 594-600.
163 Zafarana (1976), 235-236.
164 Roest (2000), 171.
165 Cantini (1934), 41-42.
166 Dumitrescu (2013).
167 Phillips (2009).

this emphasis on experience and adaptation to actual circumstances as essential to developing effective communication skills.

Rhetoric emerged as another key area of pedagogical adaptation. Medieval educators recognized the importance of adjusting the principles of religious rhetoric to address the needs of a more socially diverse audience, which included both lay and religious groups.[168] For example, some authors believed that the vernacular could be used in the service of Christian education and pastoral work.[169] The circulation of preachers, who helped to develop new forms of address that were better suited to the changing times, facilitated this adjustment. In addition to rhetoric, dialectics was also adapted to meet the demands of spiritual growth.[170] The *agon* or struggle inherent in educational dialogues permeates the scenes of instruction in many English medieval texts.[171] By emphasizing the adaptation to the public and not the logic of argumentation, educators sought to reform teaching practices and make them more relevant to the needs of their students. This phenomenon was particularly evident in the handling of individual topics, where educators broke with their predecessors' approaches and developed flexible methods of instruction. For instance, Latin textbooks were preferred because they were more engaging due to their dramatic and even violent content.[172]

Late medieval teachers accommodated the knowledge transmitted from classical writers to the formation of rules for composition.[173] They recognized the value of the rhetorical principles established by ancient authorities like Aristotle, Cicero, and Quintilian, but also understood the need to modify and expand upon these ideas to suit the requirements of their own disciples. For instance, the Franciscan Guibert of Tournai, in his thirteenth-century treatise *Eruditio regum et principum*, drew on Ciceronian rhetorical precepts but adapted them to offer guidance on the art of preaching, letter-writing, and other forms of discourse relevant to medieval life.[174] Similarly, the English rhetorician Geoffrey of Vinsauf, in his influential *Poetria nova*, built upon the foundation of classical rhetoric but focused on the specific challenges of poetic composition, providing detailed advice on topics such as amplification, ornamentation, and

---

168 Menache and Horrowitz (2016).
169 Chardonnens&Bryan (2012) and Copeland (1991).
170 Dumitrescu (2018).
171 Dumitrescu (2018), 5.
172 Dumitrescu (2018), 62.
173 Davenport (2004).
174 Roest (2000), 187-188.

the effective use of figures of speech.[175] By borrowing, changing, and supplementing the rhetorical lore of the ancients, medieval teachers like Guibert and Geoffrey could create new systems of composition.

Franciscan Observance too tapped into the power of adaptive practices in medieval education. The Italian Observants, under the authority of Bernardino da Siena, established a *Studium Moralis Theologiae* at Monteripido to train preachers and confessors in practical theology and the *casus conscientiae*.[176] The intense mobility of Observant preachers underpinned the practice of addressing different people and the attempt to find methods and ideas that would fit more than one group. Preachers like James of the Marches, who traveled extensively through Europe exemplify this mobility. John Capistrano also conducted extensive preaching tours in the German lands between 1451 and 1456. By departing from the rigid Aristotelianism and scholasticism that had previously dominated the field, the Observants created a more flexible system of instruction, both moral and general. This shift became apparent in Bernardino of Siena's *Pro Scholaribus Septem Disciplinae*, where he advocated for a balanced education that encompasses scripture, the arts of the trivium, and practical sciences, aiming to equip friars for effective ministry.[177] This adaptability became evident in a wide range of educational practices, from adjusting genres like biography and epistolography to creating new forms of address and argumentation.

Chronicles responded to the practices of adaptation, abbreviation, and compilation which further shaped the transmission and reception of historical knowledge. Nicholas Glassberger, for example, remarked that the *studium generale* of Paris came to be known as *infernus* due to its moral laxity and financial burdens, claiming that Observant friars could not study there while adhering to the purity of the Franciscan rule.[178] This suggests

---

175 Martin (1988).
176 Bistoni (1973).
177 Bernardino of Siena, *Pro Scholaribus Septem Disciplinae*, 406-408: Ego sitienti dabo de fonte aque vite gratis// Inpossibile enim est pervenire ad perfectionem cuiusque studii et scientie, nisi ante precedat magna extimatio altitudinis eius; est separatio, scilicet ab omni distractivo extrinseco.
178 Glassberger, *Chronica*, 297: Observantes studere vellent et desiderarent, sed conqueri de hoc merito deberent, quod ipsi de communitate omnes conventus, in quibus habet ordo studium generale, vellunt ipsi habere et nullum Observantibus dare, nec ipsi vellent permittere, quod ibi promoverentur ad studia, sed promotiones darent illis de sua vita. sed et propter innumerabiles dissolutiones, quae multo adhuc amplius vigent in conventibus studiorum generalium, sicut parisius testatur locus, qui dicitur infernus, propter inhonestates tacendas, ne aures audientium tinnire contingeret, et propter exactiones pecuniarias ampliores quam apud saeculares, multaque alia tacenda; dicebant se cum puritate regulae non posse ibi studere.

that Glassberger tailored his writings to highlight the perceived failings of Conventual institutions and to bolster the legitimacy of the Observant movement. In addition, Franciscan chroniclers sometimes destroyed older sources in an effort to create a more uniform and coherent narrative of Franciscan history. For example, Bonaventure ordered the destruction of earlier constitutions and *vitae* of Francis of Assisi in order to promote his own vision of the order.[179] This practice of destroying older sources highlights the importance that Franciscan chroniclers placed on shaping the transmission and reception of historical knowledge.

Chroniclers adjusted their sources to suit the specific needs and interests of their intended audience, abbreviated voluminous histories into more manageable forms, and compiled disparate sources into coherent narratives. A prime example of this practice is Paolino Veneto's *Satirica rerum gestarum*, which combines a universal chronicle with a variety of preaching tools, including distinction collections, sayings, and geographical and mythological lore. This practice of compiling diverse sources into unified narratives points to a commitment to presenting a comprehensive and engaging account of their history.[180] These techniques were essential in creating effective narratives that communicated the sequence of events clearly and compellingly for their monastic audiences. Chroniclers often faced the challenge of bridging literacy and orality by capturing the nature of oral narratives within the confines of the written word and employing strategies such as vivid language, dialogue, and characterization. This bridged the gap between literacy and orality, conveying historical experience to a diverse audience. As portrayed in chronicles, Observant preachers frequently employed vivid imagery and rhetorical devices to make religious teachings more accessible and memorable for their audiences. Chroniclers praised Bernardino da Siena for his "picturesque and evocative exempla" and his "theatrical rhetorical elements."[181] These techniques helped to bring biblical stories and moral teachings to life for his listeners, making them more relatable and engaging.

The style of adaptation was driven by factors such as cultural and linguistic particularities, and ideological and theological positions. A telling case was that of female convent scribes who worked on Franciscan chronicles, demonstrating that nuns were engaged readers who interacted with the material, molding it to suit their spiritual needs and those of

---

179 Roest (2000), 9.
180 Roest (2000), 288.
181 Roest (2000), 310.

their communities. In sum, much of the Observant success in effective communication hinged on their ability to adapt to rules and to adjust a topic to distinct milieux.[182]

II.2.2. Between devotion and education

The above remarks show the Observants developing a comprehensive approach to education that promoted their pastoral mission. Their formation began in the convent through daily practices of preaching, devotion, liturgical observance, and private study, activities that shaped not only novices but friars at all stages of spiritual development.[183] Alongside preaching, Observant friars engaged in a spectrum of pastoral activities aimed at teaching the fundamentals of Christian worship and moral principles. Contemporary chroniclers documented this educational dimension, particularly noting the contributions of *doctores theologiae*.[184] This educational effort targeted society as a whole, while focusing on specific areas deemed strategic for the success of their pastoral mission. Even if no novel or exclusive to the Observant movement, these pastoral efforts aligned with the guidelines established in the aftermath of the Fourth Lateran Council, which emphasized preaching and mandated annual confession as essential components of a comprehensive pastoral strategy.[185]

The relationship between tradition and innovation in Observant education merits careful analysis. While the movement built upon established educational frameworks, the degree to which it developed distinctive approaches remains a crucial question. Such an investigation requires examining both the Observants' pedagogical methods and their self-perception as educators. Religious movements that idealized the past often exhibited a combination of issues of preservation and transformation. Indeed, the Observant approach might best be understood as either innovative restoration or conservative innovation – two frameworks that capture this dynamic tension. As Giovanni Grado Merlo observed, regarding the Franciscans, "apparently, everything was new and, at the same time, everything seemed old."[186]

---

182 Datsko (1995).
183 Delcorno (2015), 150.
184 Glassberger, *Chronicle*, 311: Anno Domini 4443 fuit minister generalis 1 frater Mathias Frater Doring, sacrae theologiae doctor, in ohedientia papae Felicis, id Mathias Doring est in partibus citramonlanis
185 Debby (2001).
186 Delcorno (2015), 148

Ever since their beginnings, the Franciscans had nuanced views on learning. While Saint Francis had misgivings about learning for its own sake and privileged humility, as noted, he welcomed learned friars who showed knowledge. Francis expected friars to live in perfection according to their capacities, allowing existing friars to continue studying if it aligned with poverty and prayer. His invitation to Anthony of Padua to teach in Bologna demonstrates that Francis promoted learning when it was integrated with religious ideals.[187]

The Observants also tried to solve this challenge of balancing the demands of devotion and education. As they sought to renew the order's commitment to the ideals of poverty, humility, and prayer, they also addressed the problem of how to integrate learning and scholarship into their religious life. This tension between the contemplative and the intellectual dimensions of the Franciscan vocation was a source of ongoing debate and controversy within the Observant movement, as it defined the proper role of education in their pursuit of spiritual perfection.

The Observants spearheaded the efforts at catechesis and moral formation, connecting the strict adherence to law with a cultivated spirit of repentance and observance among the laity. This educational and moral project transcended the order's commitments, intersected with humanist currents, and occasionally sparked innovation. Symbolic acts like the bonfires of the vanities served not only to destroy material symbols of pride and luxury but also to etch the moral drama of renunciation into the collective memory. Reformers employed a range of tools, including vernacular treatises, instructional letters, images, paintings, processions, and theater, all aimed at saving souls by reorienting clergy and laity towards their obligations and deepening their commitment to and understanding of lay Christian life.[188]

The chronicles serve as key documents revealing the tension between the value of secular learning and religious devotion.[189] The argument which Bernardino Aquilano makes in chapter twelve of his *Chronicle*, is that whereas the Order might benefit from secular studies, its primary focus should remain on spiritual matters. His observation reflected a debate about the role of religious orders in the educational system and the

---

187 Roest (2000), 3.
188 Mixson (2015).
189 Aquilano, *Chronicle*, 43-44.

balance between secular and religious knowledge.[190] Aquilano's *Chronicle* touches on debates about integrating learning while maintaining strict observance of poverty and prayer. Scholarly rigor was not unanimously agreed upon, as the tradition of mendicant poverty emphasized spiritual devotion over scholarly attainment. For some, maintaining this emphasis on prayer and worship was seen as preferable to incorporating rigorous study. However, others argued that a higher level of learning was necessary to equip the friars to defend and spread their message to both church and society.[191] This suggests debates around balancing the ideal of total poverty against effectively carrying out preaching and pastoral duties, with Aquilano's *Chronicle* highlighting concerns that extensive studies could compromise their exemplary piety and simplicity if taken too far.

II.2.3. Observant mentors: Bernardino of Siena, John Capistrano, and their educational activities

Central to the Observant educational activities in the framework of reform was the role of Observant mentors, the exemplary figures who were recognized to embody the Observant ideals. First, Bernardino of Siena attracted large crowds to embrace a life of poverty and devotion. His sermons, which focused on the importance of moral reform and the need to resist worldly temptations, resonated with the Observant ideal of spiritual renewal.[192] His personal example of humility, asceticism, and commitment to the Franciscan Rule served as a model for his fellow Observants to emulate.[193]

As Bernardino became a force to be reckoned with, his sermons shaped the religious landscape of his time. He treated each of the sins that plagued social classes, from peasants to the most illustrious noble. The crowd listened, as he railed against the "bad habits" and superstitions that corrupt their hearts, the petty rivalries that tore their communities asunder, and the ostentatious displays of heraldry that fed their vanity. Bernardino's message was a call to renounce earthly temptations. He painted a vivid picture of a society in the grip of demonic forces, where the only path to salvation lay in strict adherence to true religion. His words struck a chord, and soon the cities of Italy were filled with moral rules about every aspect of daily life, from clothes to food.[194] Like him, other

---

190 Aquilano, *Chronicle*, 43-44.
191 Aquilano, *Chronicle*, 45.
192 Mormando (1999), 200
193 Mormando (1999), 155-163.
194 Mormando (1999).

Observants were at the forefront of this movement shaping society to their vision of piety and order. Their sermons and treatises offer a window into a world in flux, where the old certainties were crumbling and new ways of being were struggling to appear. However, these projects of moral reform were embraced only by a few outside the Observant circles.[195]

The decisive influence of Bernardino of Siena prompted the Italian friars to abandon the initial reservations about the role of education within the Franciscan Observance. Bernardino emphasized the necessity of a solid cultural formation for effective preachers, driving the Observants from the solitude of hermitages to the cities and their outskirts.[196] This shift led to establishing numerous new Observant friaries, that, in turn, engendered a closer relationship with urban society and its authorities.

This transformation placed the effectiveness of pastoral action at the heart of the Observant religious identity, requiring a better-organized educational system. Alongside Biblical studies, the Observants prioritized moral theology and canon law, viewing these disciplines as effective means of preparing expert preachers and confessors. The growing importance of canon law is evident in the biographies of prominent Observant figures like Bernardino of Siena, John Capistrano, and Bernardino of Feltre.[197] For instance, while preaching in Vicenza, Bernardino of Siena "took books of canon law with him to the pulpit and read the decretals publicly," while Capistrano, in his sermons, described canon law as the quintessence or winepress of theology (medulla/tocular theologiae). This emphasis on canon law has led to the characterization of Capistrano as "a jurist in the pulpit."[198]

Moreover, the study of moral theology and canon law equipped preachers with specific skills to engage in political debates within cities and states at large. This combination of disciplines was reflected in the pastoral guidelines produced by Franciscan Observant friars, as evidenced by works such as the *Summa angelica de casibus conscientiae* by Angelo Carletti and the model sermon collections of Michele Carcano.[199]

Furthermore, the evolution of the fifteenth-century Observant constitutions highlights the centrality of studies in relation to preaching. Initially, in 1430, study guidelines were part of the order's internal life chapter. However, by 1443, the school system was discussed within the

---

195 Mixson (2015).
196 Mormando (1999), 33.
197 Romagnoli (2011).
198 Mixson (2015b), 82.
199 Delcorno (2015), 155.

context of preaching, as outlined in the ninth chapter of the Franciscan *Regula Bullata*, with the explicit aim of shaping both preachers and confessors. This shift marked the rise of pastoral and political missions as defining aspects of the Franciscan Observance *sub vicariis* identity. The emphasis on instruction in the *Regula Bullata* also marked a shift in priorities, with preaching superseding poverty. This renewed identity aligned with Bonaventure's propositions from the 1260s, which justified studying as a means to fulfill the rule's explicit mandate for friars to preach. This was meant to illustrate Bonaventure's assertion that the Franciscans were the true *ordo fratrum praedicatorum*.[200]

The other major "pillar of Observance," John Capistrano, also brought up the dichotomy between learning and spiritual progress. In the *Life of Capistrano*, Christopher of Varese details John's preoccupation for *scientia* and books, in parallel with his emphasis on the importance of spiritual exercises, prayer, and meditation for novices.[201] He outlined a regimen of practices aimed at fostering self-knowledge and religious discipline. This included meditation on various religious themes, regular confession, daily prayer, and weekly physical discipline. Novices were also encouraged to engage in another daily hour of mental prayer to deepen their self-understanding and knowledge of God. These instructions, reminiscent of earlier Franciscan models and the monastic tradition, aimed to cultivate the religious self through precise practices. However, Capistrano's approach differed in its emphasis on the strict control of imagery, both in meditation models and the use of confession to eliminate empty *phantasias*.[202]

Although not explicitly revealed in the sources, Capistrano's interest in education surfaces at several moments, like in one of his letters, where he made a seemingly mundane request: the transfer of "expensive books" to Hamburg, where they were to be chained to the shelves of the convent library.[203] This small request placed at the end of a missive,

---

200 Delcorno (2015), 156.
201 Christopher Varese, *Vita Capestrani*, 114.
202 Delcorno (2015), 153.
203 Glassberger, *Chronicle*, 289.

speaks about the relationship between Observants and studies.[204] Even as the Observants emphasized the virtues of simplicity and detachment from worldly concerns, they could not escape the notion that their mission required a certain level of intellectual preparation.

Once again, the episode shows how the Observants found themselves caught between two competing ideals: the "innocentissima simplicitas" of the eremitic life, and the rigorous demands of pastoral ministry. For some, the solution lay in a kind of studied austerity, a life of the mind that was nevertheless grounded in the virtues of poverty and humility. For others, however, the very notion of academic study was a distraction from the true path of spiritual perfection. This tension is nowhere clearer than in the "querimoniae" sent by a group of French Observants to the Council of Constance in 1415. They decried the emphasis on logic and philosophy, arguing that it led to vainglory and a neglect of the communal life of the convent. They also lamented that the friars enjoy less the narrative of Saint Francis' *Life* than the texts of Aristotle, adding that anyone who dared to place the saint's life and doctrine before them would be met with nothing but derision.[205]

Yet even as they railed against the excesses of learning, the Observants could not escape its influence entirely. Their critique was itself steeped in the language and concepts of medieval scholasticism, a proof of the pervasive influence of the university on the intellectual life of the time. The role of study as a means to achieve pastoral goals became a point of contention, sparking debates that would shape the character of the

---

204 Capistrano letter in Glassberger, *Chronicle*: Rogans etiam vos, ut velitis esse contenti in his, qui vobis nomine meo assignabuntur nec alios impedire, mittatisque quamprimum ad me duos fratres idoneos propter aliqua expedientia ad commoditatem loci Ambergensis. Assignabo enim eis quosdam pretiosos libros pro eodem loco deputatos, in libraria quamprimum catenandos, iuxta voluntatem donatoris. Mittatis etiam mihi, si placet, per eosdem fratres aliquas bonas candelas; quodque ut faciatis, etiam atque etiam rogo. Fratri Christophoro praefato, socio meo fidelissimo, in omnibus meo nomine explicandis fidem indubiam adhibere dignemini, sicut mihi ipsi, commendans vobis illum una cum aliis Viennam profecturis sicut animam meam. Et si opportunum fuerit, mittatis secum duos fratres usque ad Ratisbonam. Novembris 1452. *I also ask you to be content with those who are assigned to you in my name and not hinder others, and send as soon as possible two suitable brothers for some expedient for the convenience of the place of Amberg. For I will assign to them some precious books designated for the same place, to be chained in the library as soon as possible, according to the donor's wishes. Also, if it pleases you, send through the same brothers some good candles to me; and I ask this again and again. And may you deign to show unwavering trust to Brother Christopher, my aforesaid faithful companion, in all matters explained in my name, just as I myself commend him to you, along with others going to Vienna, as my own soul. And if it should be opportune, send with them two brothers as far as Ratisbon. Farewell.*
205 Delcorno (2015), 154.

movement for generations to come. While the Italian Observants under the vicars (*sub vicariis*) and the Ultramontane Observant provinces embraced the necessity of intellectual formation, this stance was not universally accepted. Opposition to the emphasis on study was vehement, as evidenced by Lope de Salazar's later *Segundas satisfacciones* (1460), and the tension between the contemplative eremitical life and a life of pastoral action posed a persistent challenge for the Observants, one that struck at the very heart of their identity as followers of Saint Francis.

This conflict came to a head in the aftermath of John Capistrano's promulgation of new constitutions for the Observants. Faced with resistance among the friars *sub vicariis*, which he described as a "rebellionis pertinacia," Capistrano found himself compelled to issue a letter, *De studio promovendo* (1444), in which he reaffirmed the necessity of studies and a proper school system. Capistrano's letter was a blend of rhetorical skill and theological acumen. He argued that contempt for learning was not only contrary to human nature but also a rejection of the Holy Spirit's gifts. In making this case, he defended a shift in the character of the Franciscan religious family, one that he presented as an improvement.[206]

In their turn, the chronicles reflect the Observants' vacillation between instruction and spiritual contemplation. Glassberger's chronicle reveals the figure of John Capistrano as an efficient recruiter of new students:

> Beatus autem pater Iohannes de Capistrano tantum fructum fecit in civitate Lipsia praedicando, quod multos magistros et studentes, numero LX, ad Ordinem recepit, e quibus XXXIY per venerabilem patrem fratrem Christophorum de Varisio ad conventum Norimbergensem per Bambergam, datis ad Episcopum litteris, transmisit. Et Norimbergae manserunt X, videlicet frater Iohannes Xantes, frater Iohannes Gratia, frater Rufinus etc.; reliqui transmissi sunt Viennam ad conventum sancti Theobaldi. Inter quos fuerunt frater Cherubinus Saxo et frater Aegidius de Salice, qui postea fuit Guardianus in Cosla et demum ante divisionem trium Provinciarum rediit ad istam Provinciam et multis annis fuit confessor Clarissarum et Norimbergae obiit.

> The blessed father John Capistrano achieved such great success preaching in the city of Leipzig that he received many masters and students, numbering 60, into the Order, of whom 34 were sent through Bamberg

---

[206] Delcorno (2015), 158 which cites Capistrano's words: *Date mihi veniam, si placet, quia ad meliora charismata vos promovere curavi.*

to the Nuremberg convent by the venerable father brother Christopher of Varese, with letters given to the Bishop. And 10 remained in Nuremberg, namely brother John Xantes, brother John Gratia, brother Rufinus, etc.; the rest were sent to Vienna to the convent of Saint Theobald. Among them were brother Cherubinus the Saxon and brother Aegidius de Salice, who later became Guardian in Kosla and finally, before the division of the three Provinces, returned to this Province and for many years was confessor to the Poor Clares and died in Nuremberg.[207]

Glassberger reveals Capistrano's vision of educating the young in a letter which he sent to the community in Leipzig and which shows the connection between instruction and the spread of the Observance.[208] It is worth having a look at the entire text for, by including this letter in his chronicle, Glassberger reveals John of Capistrano's vision for educating young novices who played a vital role in the spread of the Observant movement. Capistrano's guidelines and recommendations correlate instruction and the growth of the Observance. He begins by expressing his intention to increase the size of the Leipzig community by sending them young novices of moral character and competent education:

> Cupiens familiam vestram augmentare, quemadmodum pollicitus fueram, per fratrem Christophorum, socium meum, nonnullos novitios, iuvenes quidem bonae indolis et competentis litteraturae, ad Religionem aptissimos, nullo penitus defectu impeditos, ad vos dirigo.

> Desiring to increase your family, as I had promised, through my brother Christopher, my companion, I direct to you some novices, young men indeed of good character and adequate learning, most suitable for the religious life, entirely unimpeded by any defect.[209]

Then, he emphasizes the importance of appointing a devoted preceptor to guide these novices during their novitiate, ensuring they receive a strong foundation and beginning in their religious life:

> quibus, rogo, velitis aliquem bonum et devotum praeceptorem constituere, ut in eorum novitiatu bonum suscipiant fundamentum et principium.

---

207   Glassberger, *Chronicle*, 342.
208   Also discussed in Delcorno (2015), 151.
209   Glassberger, *Chronicle*, 342.

> To them I ask that you might be willing to appoint some good and devout instructor, so that they may receive a good foundation and beginning in their novitiate.[210]

Capistrano argues that if the novices are nurtured in a highly moral manner, they will not only benefit themselves but also contribute to the spiritual growth of others, inspiring him to send more novices in the future:

> Nam si religiosissime fuerint enutriti, non solum sibi, sed et aliis proficere possunt, animaborque ego ad alios mittendum.

> For if they are raised in the most religious manner, they can not only benefit themselves but also others, and I will be encouraged to send more.[211]

The letter then revelas the specific items for the novices' education. Capistrano acknowledges the value of learning to sing, but, at the same time, he prioritizes the cultivation of a contemplative and penitential spirit, encouraging the novices to learn to weep and devote themselves to prayer:

> Placet mihi, quod novitii discant cantare, magis tamen placeret, ut discerent plorare et orationi vacare: quia quotidie cantare parit vobis Fratrum penuriam, mentem vagam deducit et adeo tempus consumit, ut nullus vestrum evadere possit in officio praedicandi clarus et peritus; propter quod magna sequitur animarum iactura.

> It pleases me that the novices learn to sing, yet it would be more pleasing if they learned to weep and devote themselves to prayer, because singing daily causes a lack of seriousness among you, distracts the mind, and consumes so much time that none of you can excel in the duty of preaching, clear and proficient; for which reason there follows a great loss of souls.[212]

He cautions against excessive singing, as it may lead to a scarcity of friars, a distracted mind, and a lack of proficiency in preaching, resulting in a loss of souls. Instead, he recommends restricting singing to the Mass and vespers. Moreover, Capistrano stresses the importance of the master

---

210 Glassberger, *Chronicle*, 342.
211 Glassberger, *Chronicle*, 342.
212 Glassberger, *Chronicle*, 342.

exhorting and teaching the novices to meditate on Christ's passion, their own misery, the day of death, the pains of hell, their past sins, and the glory promised to them:

> Item, quod magister saepenumero hortetur novitios suos doceatque meditari passionem Christi, propriam miseriam, diem mortis, infernales poenas, propria peccata perpetrata et gloriam eis promissam. Item, quod novitii bis saltem in hebdomada confiteantur, revelando malas phantasias et cogitationes, ut tentati ad vomitum non redeant.
>
> Likewise, let the master frequently exhort his novices to meditate on the passion of Christ, their own misery, the day of death, the infernal torments, the sins they have committed, and the promised glory. Also, let the novices confess at least twice a week, revealing evil fantasies and thoughts, so that when tempted, they do not fall back into sin.[213]

He advises the novices to confess at least twice a week, revealing their fantasies and thoughts to avoid succumbing to temptation. The letter also prescribes daily devotional practices, such as reciting the prayers to the Virgin Mary with seven meditations and genuflections. He then provides detailed instructions for each meditation, focusing on key events in the life of Christ and the Virgin Mary.[214]

Capistrano places a premium on proper discipline and austerity, stating that only prelates should mortify the novices and that the master should lead by example.[215] He condemns the practice of disciplining novices or other friars, except in cases of incorrigibility or grave offenses.[216] The letter also addresses the issue of secular persons dining with the friars, which

---

213   Glassberger, *Chronicle*, 343.
214   Glassberger, *Chronicle*, 343. Item, quod singulis diebus faciant coronam Virginis Mariae cum VII meditationibus, sicut VII sunt paries ipsius coronae, et cum genuflexione, dum dicunt Iesus. *Also, let them make the crown of the Virgin Mary with the seven meditations every day, as there are seven beads in the crown itself, and with a genuflection while saying 'Jesus'.*
215   Glassberger, *Chronicle*, 343. Item, quod nullus fratrum audeat mortificare novitios praeter Praelatos, et quidquid magister eos edocet, ipse primo faciat. *Moreover, let no brother dare to discipline the novices except the superiors, and whatever the master teaches them, let him do it first himself.*
216   Glassberger, *Chronicle*, 343. Nam nullo pacto frater disciplinari debet, nisi sit incorrigibilis feccritque aliquod magnum delictum. *For by no means should a brother be disciplined unless he is incorrigible or has committed some grave offense.*

Capistrano vehemently opposed.[217] He remarks that one should rather eat bread and onions than permit to seculars to dine with the friars, even if it means losing the offerings they bring.[218]

The letter concludes with additional instructions, such as prohibiting novices from wearing white tunics to differentiate themselves from the Conventuals, setting aside an hour for mental prayer, and reiterating the importance of avoiding secular dining companions and allowing novices to discipline themselves.[219] Capistrano's letter to the Leipzig community thus reveals the opportunities but also the limitations of promoting education in the spread of the Observant movement. By providing detailed pedagogical guidelines for the instruction and spiritual formation of novices, Capistrano seems to encourage a category of Observants embodying the spirit of Saint Francis' austerity.[220] Concurrently, he emphasizes cultivating a contemplative and penitential lifestyle, proper discipline, and the need to maintain a distinct identity from the Conventuals and secular society.

The role of education in the Observant movement surfaces even more clearly in the attempts to institutionalize instruction. If in the beginning, the Franciscan *studium* network appears like a simplified Dominican system,[221] later, the Observants included stipulations about education in official documents like the *Constitutiones Martinianae* and Capistrano's 1443 *Constitutions*. The 1430 *Constitutiones Martinianae*, which the same John Capistrano helped formulate, emphasized the papal expectations for Observant preaching. Preachers were to avoid criticizing the higher clergy and focus on arming the people against the dangers of

---

217 Glassberger, *Chronicle*, 343. Item, quod introductio saecularium personarum ad mensam sicut diabolus evitetur. Si quidam saeculares scandalizarentur, dicite, quia ego dixi et scripsi vobis. *Also, let the introduction of secular persons at the table be avoided like the devil. If some seculars should be scandalized, tell them that I have said and written to you.*

218 Glassberger, *Chronicle*, 343. Fugite, fratres, saecularium consortium et amate solitudinem. Credite mihi, quanto magis saeculares fugietis, sicut dicebat beatus Pater noster Franciscus, tanto magis ipsi vos devotione et caritate amplectentur. *Flee, brothers, the company of seculars and love solitude. Believe me, the more you flee from seculars, as our blessed Father Francis used to say, the more they will embrace you with devotion and love.*

219 Glassberger, *Chronicle*, 343. Item, quod novitii nullo modo portent tunicas albas, quia iam Conventuales non aliud deferunt; conveniuntque praeterea nobiseum in colore concordare. *Also, let the novices by no means wear white tunics, as the Conventuals do not wear anything else; and furthermore, it is fitting that they should match us in color.*

220 Glassberger, *Chronicle*, 343. Quae omnia si observata fuerint, una cum aliis necessariis familia vestra decorabitur dilatabiturque numero et virtutibus. Vos itaque hi eritis, quales esse debent veri imitatores pauperis Francisci. *If all these things are observed, along with other necessary matters, your family will be adorned and expanded in number and virtues. Therefore, you shall be such as true imitators of poor Francis should be.*

221 Roest (2000), 5.

heretics, specifically targeting the Hussite heresy. In the 1443 constitutions, written almost entirely by Capistrano and approved by the Pope in 1449, preaching was regarded as the ultimate solution to pastoral challenges. The text describes preaching as the foundation of the Christian faith, the light of truth, the school of virtues, the destruction of vices, the way to salvation, the return of sinners, and the instruction of rational people, etc.[222] From this perspective, education among the Observants appears as primarily oriented towards effective pastoral action.

However, the Observance promoted by Capistrano in his private letters or in the constitutions was not the only type of Franciscan Observance being practiced. The interactions between various political and religious actors at the local level played a role in defining what constituted a "real" Observant religious life, suggesting that the implementation of this educational vision may have varied depending on the specific context.[223] In Poland, in the second half of the fifteenth century, for instance, the Observants prioritized structured forms of writing, especially those governed by the order given through the alphabet. They focused on labor and evangelization among the common people, delivering sermons not only in churches but also in public gathering places. This outreach effort required the use of mnemonic techniques among the Order's members, a practice that was dominant during this period.[224]

Thus, it appears that, for preachers like Capistrano, the pursuit of poverty was subordinate to the efficacy of mission and the project of reforming society. This functional approach to learning, however, was not the only path available to the Observants. As their relationship with humanistic culture would demonstrate, there were additional ways of navigating the tension between contemplation and action, between the demands of the enclosed monastic community and the conditions of a changing world. In the end, the debate over the role of instruction in the Franciscan Observance was more than an academic dispute: it became also a struggle for the essence of the movement. And while the outcome of that struggle would have far-reaching consequences for the future of the Observants, it was a strong reminder that the path to spiritual perfection was not a straight line.

---

222   Delcorno (2015), 152.
223   Roest (2000), 15.
224   Wojcik (2009), 132.

II.2.4. Education and humanism

The Observants' dedication to learning, preaching, and education positioned them as contenders to rival cultural movements, including Humanism, which had emerged as a departure from traditional university education. Humanists, including figures like Petrarch, emphasized the *studia humanitatis*, a focus on liberal arts and humanities, over the conventional legal and canonical studies. These scholars, often outside formal academic institutions, gained cultural legitimacy through education and civic service. Notable masters like Vittorino of Feltre and Guarino of Verona established innovative schools near courts in Mantua and Ferrara. Meanwhile, in republican Florence, thinkers like Coluccio Salutati and Leonardo Bruni championed civil virtue, defending urban liberty against the ambitions of other rich families. In many literary circles, Florentine and non-Florentine humanists gathered, drawing inspiration from Dante, Petrarch, and Boccaccio. This intellectual circle blended patriotism with secularized studies, exemplified by Poggio Bracciolini and Giannozzo Manetti.[225]

The Church reacted in various ways to the humanist culture, with the papacy accepting the innovative program of study and contributing to the growth of the *studia humanitatis*. Religious orders, however, showed occasional hostility towards humanism, perceiving the disruptive potential of philological studies and the competition of new pedagogical models. Nevertheless, religious figures like Ambrogio Traversari, engaged in a substantial dialogue with humanists within the schools and sought to use elements from classical culture to their advantage.[226]

The Humanists maintained a complex relationship with the Observants, oscillating between acceptance and rejection. Italian Renaissance scholars, like Poggio Bracciolini, opposed the Observant way of life, perceiving their increasing influence as a threat to a vision of cultural revival through the lens of antiquity. Poggio portrayed the mendicants as unlearned and unsophisticated, asserting their own erudition in contrast. They viewed the mendicants as a reflection of the obstacles to attaining knowledge, while positioning themselves as the harbingers of progress and the future of knowledge.[227] Yet, if the dichotomy between theology and *philosophia gentilum* shaped approaches like Poggio's, Humanists held more positive views. They often engaged in dialogue, as for instance Coluccio Salutati, a

---

225   Mixson (2015a), 35.
226   Mixson (2015), 37.
227   Mixson (2016b), 113.

Florentine Renaissance humanist, who, even if a fervent admirer of classical works, argued that an ascetic contemplative life was more valuable than a secular life of civic engagement. Other prominent humanists, including Petrarch, explored the ideal way to lead a devout life, emphasizing spiritual tranquility achieved through meditation and prayer. Petrarch, who was perceived as bearing a Franciscan influence, admired the Carthusians for their asceticism and their association of piety with philosophy and learning, seeing them as potential promoters of classical scholarship. For his part, Coluccio and his associates sought to strike a balance between contemplation and active life, a notion shared by thinkers like Giannozo Manetti, Niccolò Niccoli, Roberto Rossi, and Marsilio Ficino. This idea of a *vita mixta*, developed by Jordan of Quedlinburg and adopted by Luigi Marsili, Andrea Biglia, and Giles of Viterbo, aimed at dismantling the barriers between convents and the world.[228]

The relations between Humanists and Observants received further impetus in their shared interest in the culture of antiquity. Although with the Humanists this interest was definitely visible, the Franciscans, like the Dominicans, maintained close contact with classical texts, a tendency which intensified in the fourteenth century. Churches like Santa Maria Novella in Florence housed collections of ancient authors and reading works by Cicero, Horace, Virgil, Seneca and Latin grammarians were not uncommon. Besides, friars engaged in correspondence and debates with prominent Humanists like Pico della Mirandola and members of the Medici family. As a matter of fact, the Franciscans' activities in Florence contributed to the activities of the Florentine Academy, and their cooperation with Humanists extended well into the sixteenth century.[229]

The connections between Franciscans and Humanists went beyond intellectual debates, encompassing social life as well. Franciscan convents played a role in urban society, with institutional ties mirroring personal contacts between the mendicants and the population. In Italy, city authorities treated convent libraries as public resources with monasteries recruiting candidates for higher positions in the church from prominent families. Brothers were entrusted with instructing the young, awarded teaching positions at the city's *studium*, and dispatched as ambassadors to various tribunals.[230]

---

228 Mixson (2016b), 134.
229 Navone (1994).
230 Mixson (2016b), 116.

Such connections with powerful families shaped the dynamics of religious contemplation and *studia humanitatis*, as exemplified by the prior of Santo Spirito, who came from a noble Florentine family.[231] Lay elites of the fourteenth and fifteenth centuries, who sought to fashion a spiritual background by considering antiquity as a model, drove this process both within and beyond the convent. The configuration of a group of scholars bridging the two worlds required various factors of generation and a common intellectual ground, which can be illustrated through the shared ideals of Franciscan poverty and Humanist rejection of the world under the influence of the Stoics, as well as a reorientation toward classical rhetoric, scholarship, economics, and politics.

Soon, the Observant forms of writing and communication began to bear traces of humanist learning. Homiletic literature adopted classical models to enhance its impact on audiences. Even more, as noted, the Observants' focus on personalities, their hagiography, and conception of sainthood, echoed Plutarchean models of biographies. Indeed, the Humanists' recovery of the Plutarchean tradition gave rise to biographies of contemporary illustrious men and women, such as the *De claris selectisque mulieribus* by Giacomo Filippo Foresti and the *Gynevera de le clare donne* by Sabadino degli Arienti.[232] Other classical models cultivated by the Humanists became also visible in the Observant circles. Pope Pius II (Eneas Silvius Piccolomini) distinguished himself as a historian, with his *Commentarii* inspired by the works of Julius Caesar. Several moral Observant texts also bore the influence of humanism, as evident in works like Leandro Alberti's *De viris illustribus ordinis praedicatorum* and Marko Marulić's *De institutione bene vivendi per exempla sanctorum*.[233]

Such contacts between Humanism and the Observance surfaced on several occasions. A telling instance of the Franciscans' engagement with Humanism came from Caritas Pirckheimer (1467-1532), the learned abbess of the Convent of Saint Clare in Nuremberg. Caritas was born into a family that valued both humanist scholarship and monastic life.[234] The convent where she later lived had a strong humanist tradition, with a substantial library, literate nuns, and Franciscan preachers and confessors involved in humanist studies. One key figure was the chronicler Nicholas Glassberger himself, who served as the convent's confessor between 1483 and 1508 and

---

231 Baron (1938).
232 Mixson (2015), 48.
233 Mixson (2015), 49.
234 Barker (1995).

encouraged the nuns, under Caritas' editorship, to produce chronicles of Franciscan history drawing on original sources.

Caritas corresponded with leading German humanists like Sixtus Tucher and her brother Willibald Pirckheimer, as her humanist learning and status enabled her to take an unusual stance during the Reformation.[235] Under her supervision, the nuns produced Latin and German versions of Glassberger's chronicle as well as their own narratives that highlighted the early history of the Order of Saint Clare and the Nuremberg convent's efforts to lead other convents into "holy observance." This reflected an Observant Franciscan perspective focused on reform and the return to the founding ideals of the order while recognizing the role of the contemporary intellectual movements.[236]

Franciscan Observant chronicles also bear the traces of contacts with Humanist culture. In the debut of his chronicle, Bernardino Aquilano reflects on the dispute between Ambroggio Traversari and Angelus da Clareno concerning the translation from Greek into Latin of John Climacus' *Ladder of Divine Ascent*.[237] Bernardino presents Angelus as one precursor of the Observance who even if he did not partake in the *scientia humanitatis* and did not pursue studies of Greek, translated the Greek text which was popular among Franciscans. Ambroggio, a famous humanist with a deep knowledge of Greek culture, however criticized the translation and produced a different one. Aquilano deplored the conflict with the humanists and suggested the need for better coordination between Observants and Humanists.

> Sed vir quidam utique religiosus vitae monasticae, nomine Ambrosius, ut aiunt vir utique in scientia humanitatis, ut vocant, apprime doctus necnon et graecae linguae eruditus, illuminet librum transtulit in latinum politiori sermone et elegantiori latino. Quod laudo; sed hoc mihi exosum est et nescio, ubi hunc eloquentiae modum didicerit servus Dei existens, quod in principio libri multas injurias illi pauperculo dicit; et unde debuisset illum laudare quasi virum bonae vitae et rectae conscientiae, qui librum illum latinis dedit, et propter ipsum infinita bona, ut ita loquar, operati sunt, vituperare conatur. Si meruit vel demeruit, ex verbis suis summus arbiter judicet. Fecit ille bonus homo, quod novit; certe si ille notitiam latinis non dedisset, forsitan adhuc ignorarent, et multis amicis Dei praestitit lumen et non minimam consolationem.

---

235   Barker (1995).
236   Barker (1995), 260.
237   Aquilano, *Chronicle*, 4-5.

But a certain religious man, indeed of the monastic life, named Ambrosius, as they say, very learned in the science of humanities, as they call it, and also educated in the Greek language, translated that book into a more polished and more elegant Latin. I praise this; but I hate and do not know where this servant of God, existing, learned this mode of eloquence, because at the beginning of the book he says many insults to that poor man; and where he should have praised him as a man of good life and right conscience, who gave that book to the Latins, and because of him in the end they did such good things, so to speak, he tries to revile him. If he deserved or did not deserve it, let the highest judge judge from his words. That good man did what he knew; certainly if he had not given knowledge to the Latins, perhaps they would still be ignorant, and he provided light and no small consolation to many friends of God.[238]

Furthermore, following the Humanist tendency to return to the past as a way of moral instruction, the Observants appear to have also used chronicles as a major tool of education. Nicholas Glassberger places this idea at the beginning of his *chronicle* where he cites the words of the famous Franciscan teacher, Nicholaus de Lyra (1270-1349), who conceived of his commentary on the *Book of Esther* as a way "to direct the memory of the past in view of future actions (memoriam praeteritorum dirigere dicit in agendis respectu futurorum).[239]" Glassberger continues by displaying his past experiences in writing for educational purposes like when he was asked to compose a brief regional chronicle on Strasbourg. On this occasion, he adds that he used a concise and simple style (*succincte stiloque simplici*), thereby echoing that the didactic aims of his historical writing unfolded at the intersection of contemporary cultural currents.[240]

II.3. Communicating the Observant reform

If education was a cornerstone for the Observants in demonstrating their values within the discourse of reform and in reinforcing their legitimacy, it was through formal and informal communication methods that the Observants effectively consolidated their position. They employed documents, sermons, and letters to articulate and disseminate their values both within the Order and to other communities. Additionally, they

---

238 Aquilano, *Chronicle*, 4.
239 Glassberger, *Chronicle*, 3.
240 Glassberger, *Chronicle*, 3.

utilized narrative forms such as chronicles or hagiographies for internal communication within the convent.

Thus, effective communication became essential to expand the Franciscan Order. The chronicles abound in episodes echoing the idea that the Observants placed a premium on communication. A case in point is Glassberger's depiction of Fredebald's role as confessor to a noblewoman, which exemplifies the importance of continuous pastoral care and spiritual guidance in the Franciscan ministry.[241] Glassberger also recounts another telling episode, this time occurring in *Theutonia*, where several Franciscan friars struggled to convey their message because of language barriers. This inability not only hindered their communication but also engendered hostility and accusations of heresy among the local population, obstructing their missionary objectives.[242] Such cases revealing the challenges of communication among the Observants, prompt a discussion of the strategies and types the Observants employed to overcome these barriers. Before turning to the chronicles as a key form of communication, in this section, I will look at the Observants' two main practices of communication: one oriented towards moralization and another pertaining to the configuration of a legal framework of the Observance.

II.3.1. Communication oriented towards moralization: preaching and life-writing

A tool of communication which the Observants used on a large scale, preaching was widespread in medieval cultural settings. It was a way of conveying a spiritual or moral message from a charismatic orator to a group of listeners. But in the later Middle Ages, a period when Humanism and the Renaissance promoted new perspectives on knowledge and life, preaching offered a mixed reception. As noted, mendicant preachers were ridiculed by Renaissance scholars like Poggio Bracciolini (1380-1459) who, nevertheless, acknowledged that they were outstanding performers and could attract large crowds.[243] Poggio's musings reflected a cleavage between a religious view that emphasized the preservation of an old form of public austere spirituality and a secular, utilitarian approach.

Despite such contestations arising in the intellectual milieu at the turn of the fifteenth century, preaching remained the cornerstone of Observants' pastoral activity. Their sermon styles took different turns according to

---

241 Glassberger, *Chronicle*, 36-37.
242 Glassberger, *Chronicle*, 11.
243 Debby (2001)

time or territory and helped them establish their authority. These styles pointed to the modulations of communication that had to be adapted to different audiences.[244] Bernardino of Siena, a faithful imitator of Saint Francis who often received recognition for his skilled oratory, emerged as the preeminent figure in the world of fifteenth-century preaching.[245] His preaching style showed mastery of exempla, linguistic sensibility, and ability to combine doctrinal exposition with narrative elements. He employed techniques, such as *postillatio* for liturgical sermons, a dramatic narrative style influenced by meditations, or the rhetorical device of *auctoritates concordantes*.[246] As scholars noted, Bernardino's sermons followed the structure of a treatise, replete with orderly distinctions and mnemonic techniques like acrostics, retrogradation, and formulas. He employed numerical symbolism, dividing his sermons into three, four, seven, or twelve parts, and employed vivid imagery inspired from natural or political spheres to visualize abstract concepts.[247]

According to his own words, Bernardino began preaching in 1412, but it was not until 1418, while preaching in Milan, that he garnered significant attention and success. Departing from the traditional "historical" sermon style and the mere presentation of basic Gospel facts, Bernardino opted for a more innovative approach, freely selecting themes that resonated with his audiences. He crafted hybrid sermon structures that blended common problems, such as marriage, with relevant Gospel readings.[248]

Following the so-called Gothic tradition of the late Middle Ages, Bernardino's preaching style adhered to the scholastic *sermo modernus* technique while adapting it to a popular style. He omitted the *prothema* used in academic sermons, added invocations to the Virgin, and aimed for a circular structure by quoting the thema at the end. Around 1412, Bernardino began to diverge from traditional preaching styles, experimenting with new rhetorical techniques and tailoring his sermons to address contemporary moral issues. Throughout the 1420s, Bernardino chose his own biblical themes rather than following the liturgy, moving away from the narrative sermon style and drawing inspiration from the Psalms, Apocalypse, and Wisdom books. He turned to exempla, appealing to different social classes with lively stories and vivid, emotional language. As scholars showed, his narrative style manifested dramatic

---

244   Murphy (1989).
245   Lappin (2000), 173.
246   Muessig (2015).
247   Muessig (2015).
248   Delcorno (1980), 444.

sensibility, using dialogues, emotional monologues, and realistic details that sometimes bordered on the comic.[249]

As noted, throughout the 1420s, Bernardino experimented with complex sermon structures, incorporating different types of subdivisions and increasing the use of *auctoritates concordantes*. His 1427 Sienese sermons achieved a balance of simplicity, elegance, and doctrinal clarity, avoiding excessive rhetorical artifice while still revealing his narrative abundance.[250] Bernardino's influence on fifteenth-century itinerant preaching cannot be overstated. His students copied his style, stories, and techniques, while other preachers widely adopted his formulae and divisions. Bernardino's sermons shaped Franciscan preaching for the years to come. However, scholars remarked that, after his death, the balanced rhetorical style he had perfected declined, as legalistic thinking, erudite classicism distorted the unity and simple eloquence of his sermons.[251]

The other pillar of Observant preaching, John Capistrano, acquired the reputation of a public speaker across many lands. He attracted massive crowds with stories about miracles and conversions. Capistrano preached not only in churches but also in public spaces like urban squares at the invitation of political leaders and was described as an old but energetic man. The fifteenth-century historian, Hartmann Schedel, described John's entrance into a new city as a striking appearance:

> We saw him in Nuremberg as [a man] of very small stature, of old age, in his sixty-fifth year of life, dry, arid, exhausted, nothing but skin, nerves, and bones, but cheerful and vigorously active.[252]

Capistrano's eloquent preaching style, characterized by dramatic descriptions of vice and virtue, captivated audiences across the continent. His preaching was further aided by reported miracles and prophecies, which strengthened his reputation. The success in converting heretics in the Austrian lands was noteworthy. His preaching in Vienna won numerous converts, and, as a result, he gained privileges and funding from Frederick III. However, as remarked, his efforts to convert Hussites in Moravia had mixed results. While he failed to achieve mass conversions,

---

249   Delcorno (1980) and Debby (2001).
250   Norman (2003).
251   Mormando (1998).
252   https://inpress.lib.uiowa.edu/feminae/DetailsPage.aspx?Feminae_ID=34911

he strengthened the loyalty of Catholic areas and rebuilding Church structures and worship.[253]

A large part of his preaching was channeled toward promoting a crusade against the Ottoman Empire which threatened to engulf Christian Europe by the middle of the fifteenth century. He saw the Ottoman conquest as a divine punishment and called for a crusade to lift the siege of Belgrade. His words raised a large crusader army, which he inspired together with John Hunyadi (1406-1456). Eventually, Capistrano's triumphant tour of preaching after the Belgrade victory in 1456 solidified his status as both a hero of Christendom and a successful preacher.[254]

Similar to preaching, life-writing in the form of hagiography conveyed models of virtue primarily for internal use among the Observants. While lives of Bernardino of Siena and John Capistrano circulated widely, biographies of other representative Observants appeared as well. Giacomo Oddi's *Specchio de l'Ordine Menore* (1474) included lives of Observant beati, many of whom lived during the period of accelerated Observant development in the fifteenth century. Two of these figures stand out: Francesco da Pavia (d.1450) whom Oddi describes struggling to reconcile the ideals of strict poverty with obedience to his superiors. Initially, he favoured a life of itinerancy and strict poverty, typical of the early Observance, but eventually came to embrace the more moderate values of the Regular Observance after experiencing divine visions. The second figure, Thoma da Firenze (d.1447), represented in Oddi's view the ideal of combining the contemplative life with active service to the Order. He embraced poverty and seclusion, yet also held positions of authority, engaged in missionary work, and preached obedience to his peers.[255]

Another prominent Observant author, Mariano da Firenze, wrote a collection of lives which focuses on the lives of less-well-known Observant beati who exemplified the virtues of contemplative poverty and seclusion. Pietro da Rieti (d.1464) was portrayed as a hermit, seeking solitude and extreme poverty, values that aligned with the strict Observance. Mariano highlights the fervent commitment to poverty of Antonio da Stroncone (d.1461) with an anecdote in which he is accused of destroying vines because of Francis' pronouncements against owning property. This example reflected the potential for conflict between strict interpretations of Franciscan poverty and the realities of communal living. Jacopo da

---

253 Mixson (2016a).
254 Mixson (2016a).
255 Lappin (2000).

Monteprandone (d.1476) is presented for his extreme asceticism, tattered habit, and miraculous powers. He represents the enduring appeal of the early Franciscan ideal of poverty and humility within the Observance.

These examples suggest that biography in the form of Observant hagiography served as a powerful internal communication tool to reinforce identity and cultivate exemplary models of virtue within the Order. Unlike preaching, which was dialogical and addressed rather external audiences, by narrating the lives of saints, beati, and other virtuous figures, hagiographies provided tangible examples of Franciscan ideals like poverty, obedience, asceticism, and spiritual devotion. Yet, like the sermons, these narratives chronicled not only individual lives but operated also as tools to align the behavior of their audiences with the values of the Observance.

II.3.2. Communication for legitimization purposes: documents and letters

Alongside preaching and life writing, communication was facilitated through other means that pertained to the formation of a coherent legal framework. The proliferation of chapter statutes, constitutions, expositions and commentaries of the Rule of Saint Francis, and other legal treatises reflects the Observant reformers' attempts to codify their vision and ensure its implementation. The *Acta capitulorum* (records of chapter meetings), letters from provincial ministers, and formularies from different Observant provinces reveal the process of communication in internal organisational matters.[256]

Following the early tumultuous leadership of Elias, who resisted the formulation of new commentaries and regulations, the Franciscan Order experienced significant changes. Commentaries, like the *Expositio Quatuor Magistrorum*, aimed to explain the Rule while acknowledging the pope's ultimate authority in interpretation. They explored questions about the application of the Rule in various contexts and deferred certain legal or moral matters to the Apostolic See. These commentaries started the categorization of the Rule's instructions into precepts and counsels, reflecting a scholastic approach to interpreting the Rule.[257]

Between 1239 and 1244, the Franciscans formulated their first constitutions and commissioned new biographical material about Francis that marked a reassessment of the Order's foundation: Francis'

---

[256] Cevins (2008) and Viallet (2014).
[257] Carta (2022).

life and his Rule. By the mid-fourteenth century, the Order had established a legal framework comprising the Rule, papal interpretations, commentaries, and constitutions. This showed a move towards a more standardized legal system, incorporating elements from other religious orders, like constitutions issued by general chapters.[258] The Observant movement produced its own commentaries and, while upholding the Rule's importance, they relied heavily on existing interpretations and authorities. As scholars showed, such commentaries functioned as vehicles for preserving and transmitting tradition rather than introducing radical new perspectives.[259]

The chronicles reflected the extensive use of these instruments, with authors holding distinct attitudes towards the importance of the communication process, inside or outside the order. Bernardino Aquilano focused on deploying the narrative and only introduced partial sermons which fitted into his scheme but did not attend so much to the letters.[260] On the contrary, in Glassberger's chronicle, letters and official documents dominated. Understandably, since Glassberger was more interested in the growth of the order beyond Italy, his chronicle extensively used decrees, like when conveying the above mentioned support in the Council of Constance for the Observant reform movement and its recognition of the Observants' role in the renewal of religious life. By using a decree to grant the Observant *custos* the power to appoint confessors and friars to assist the nuns and to inspect monasteries, the Council endorsed the Observants as agents of reform and strengthened their authority and influence. In a similar way, decrees communicated the Council's expectations for the ongoing reform or progress in individual cases like the support for the convent of the Poor Clares of Alspach under Observant guidance.[261]

Beside decrees, Glassberger privileged letters as a form of adding information from the beginning of his narrative.[262] He presents Saint Francis as an active communicator when he mentions that he, upon returning from overseas (*ultra mare*), called for a general chapter to discuss important matters affecting the Order such as the recent martyrdoms

---

258 Carta (2022).
259 Carta (2022).
260 E.g. Aquilano, *Chronicle,* 43: *Et magister Seraphiuus ait in communi sermone respondens:* « *Vere puto, quod ordo minorum nunquam in tanta fuit reputatione constitutus.*» For other references to sermons see also the references to the preaching of Robert of Lecce, Aquilano, *Chronicle,* 44-45.
261 Glassberger, *Chronicle,* 310-312.
262 Leonte (2023).

among Arab communities.²⁶³ Letters appear in addressing papacy and other Church officials as friars embarked on their far-away missions. Many of these epistles served to introduce the friars to the local clergy and lay people, and to encourage their acceptance and support.²⁶⁴ The large scale use of letters suggests the Franciscans maintained a network of communication to share information, address local issues, and maintain unity among its members.²⁶⁵

In other cases, Glassberger deploys letters as elements of religious communication during the Western Schism, as with the above mentioned allegorical and polemical letter circulated on the occasion of the Council of Pisa in 1409. The letter's critique of those perpetuating the schism and its call for unity reflect a concern within religious circles for the well-being and reform of the Church. It demonstrates that religious orders, including the Franciscans, were involved in the political and ecclesiastical debates surrounding the Western Schism. The letter's use of satire and polemic suggests that these literary techniques were part of a culture of religious communication during this period. The integration of the letter in the chronicle further underlines that Glassberger answered to the needs of an audience accustomed to a culture of textual production and dissemination within religious circles. The Observants, according to Glassberger, like other religious orders, participated in this culture by producing, copying, and distributing media related to the schism and other pressing issues facing the Church.

More illustrations about the importance of epistolary communication for spiritual purposes and for the Order's growth emerge in the initial letter-exchange between Bartholomaeus Wyer and Nicolaus Glassberger that frame the purpose and occasion for the chronicle. Glassberger expresses humility about his "imperitia" (lack of skill) and "humili rusticoque sermone" (humble and rustic speech) while also justifying that those seeking to advance in spiritual writings should seek "rectas regulas bene vivendi" (right rules for living well) rather than rhetorical polish. Scriptural quotations and allusions are woven throughout the letter, such as comparing the Franciscan order to a field blessed by God, or Francis to a foundational stone. These uses and remarks highlight the author's pursuit of genre conventions while also prioritizing content over style.

---

263 Glassberger, *Chronicle*, 17.
264 Glassberger, *Chronicle*, 12-13
265 Glassberger, *Chronicle*, 17.

Many times, letters showed versatility and became generic frames of solemn declarations and decisions. Acting as the Vicar and Commissioner of the Minister General, Bernardino of Siena shared with the Observants in Italy a set of declarations issued by Nicholas of Osimo and transmitted in epistolary form, which were examined and approved by John Capistrano, and Bernardino himself.[266] These declarations clarified aspects of the Franciscan Rule, such as the friars' obligations regarding evangelical counsels and precepts, the use of material goods, and the discernment of superfluity and curiosity. The declarations also addressed issues like the use of silver chalices and patens, consuming meat, as well as the handling of doubtful matters of theology. Through the letter, the Minister General together with Bernardino confirmed these declarations as true and in conformity with papal declarations and Franciscan institutes.[267] Concurrently, he mandated their publication under his care, pointing to the importance of epistolary frameworks for communication within the Observant movement especially in legal terms.[268]

Conclusion

By a preliminary conclusion to this section, the Observants' pursuit of reform, rooted in a desire to return to the ideals of Franciscan poverty and humility, unfolded against a backdrop of profound social, political, and intellectual transformation. The Observants' discourse of reform, as reflected in a wide range of sources, including chronicles, was shaped by their understanding of virtue. Drawing upon the established medieval discourse of virtues and vices, the Observants emphasized the practical application of virtues, poverty, obedience, and, sometimes, asceticism, as essential tools for spiritual renewal. However, sources also reveal the tensions inherent in this pursuit. Pragmatic considerations modulated the emphasis on strict observance of poverty, in their expanding pastoral mission. The virtue of obedience, while paramount, was sometimes reinterpreted to justify the Observants' separation from the Conventual Franciscans and their engagement in political activities.

The communication strategies demonstrate the Observants' navigation of power and social structures, both internally and externally. A combination of deference and assertiveness marked the Observants' relations with both ecclesiastical and secular authorities, as reflected

---

266 Glassberger, *Chronicle*, 302-305.
267 Glassberger, *Chronicle*, 303.
268 Glassberger, *Chronicle*, 305.

especially in letters and documents. While seeking papal approval and the support of powerful rulers, the Observants legitimized their own authority and to promote their vision of reform. Moreover, the types of Observant communication point in the direction of the Observants' awareness of the power of language for shaping the attitudes of the order's members. Their use of emotionally charged public rhetoric, vivid imagery, and elaborate biographical or anecdotic narratives reflects a deliberate effort to shape public perception and to mobilize support for their cause.

The Observants' commitment to education emerges as another key aspect of their reform discourse. The sources document the tensions between the Franciscan ideal of simplicity and the practical need for intellectual formation. If individual voices within the movement expressed reservations about the potential dangers of secular learning, figures like Bernardino of Siena and John Capistrano championed education for effective preaching. This led to a gradual shift within the Observant movement towards a structured approach to education, with an emphasis on moral theology, canon law, and development of rhetorical skills. The Observants' complex relationship with Humanism reflected the changes in the attitude to learning. If humanists criticized the mendicants for a perceived lack of learning, others engaged in fruitful dialogue with Observant friars, recognizing their shared interest in moral reform and pursuing knowledge. The chronicles of Bernardino Aquilano and Nicholas Glassberger bear witness to this interaction, incorporating elements of humanist rhetoric and historiography.

As demonstrated above, the Franciscan Observant discourse of reform provided a mirror of the evolving nature of religious change in the late Middle Ages. The chronicles, in particular, demonstrate how the Observants, driven by a commitment to spiritual renewal, adapted their message and methods to the specific challenges and opportunities they encountered. And, as the following section of this study will show, the two chronicles by Glassberger and Aquilano not only captured the internal dynamics of the Observant movement but also engaged with and shaped the forces that influenced the late medieval world.

III

Observant Identity and its Chronicle Forms

The above examination shows that the Franciscan Observants configured their distinctive public identity through various textual media which either presented moral advice or built the legal background of the Observance. The commitment to articulating their ideals and explaining their practices is clear not only in the sermons, rules, letters, and hagiographic biographies but also in the individual stories they circulated within the order and beyond. The following step in this analysis is to turn to the operations of the other major medium of consolidating and disseminating the Observance, the chronicles. They were aligned to the other tools of communication from which they borrowed moral tenets and documentary evidence.

With their panoramic view of the Order, the chronicles help us understand how various authors understood the challenges, innovations, and limitations in the formation of Observant identity. By narrating how the Observants dealt with both internal conflicts and external pressures while promoting their vision of an austere religious life, the chronicles not only reinforced the traditional tenets of the Observant identity but also added new elements in a distinct approach to identity formation.

As tools of communication for the order's internal use, the Observant chronicles served a triple purpose. First, they aimed at informing the monastic audience about the order (its origins, juridical grounding, and main events), allowing for a better understanding of its scope and the challenges it faced during its expansion. Second, the chronicles legitimized and solidified the Observant identity. The plethora of information and narratives was meant to make sense of seemingly disparate events that occurred across distant territories and during long time periods, weaving them into a unitary composition. Third, the Observant chronicles sought to match the discursive practices of other religious institutions like the papacy and other monastic orders who were promoting their own achievements through narratives as well. The chronicles helped the Observants gain a firm footing in the field of spiritual formation and showed their efforts to vie for attention in the public arena.

In terms of structure and composition, the late medieval Franciscan Observant chronicles, were a diverse body of historical writing that aimed to document and shape the identity of the Observant movement. They were varied in type, including comprehensive histories like Mariano da Firenze's *Compendium chronicarum Fratrum Minorum*, eyewitness accounts like Bernardino Aquilano's *Chronica Fratrum Minorum Observantiae*, and collections of biographies like Giacomo Oddi's *La Franceschina*. Besides these, several other chronicles like those by Michael of Carinthia and Eberhard Ablauff focused on a linear, chronological approach to regional events. These chroniclers framed the Observance as a providential force, chosen to restore the authentic Franciscan ideal amidst a perceived decline within the broader Order. This was achieved by selectively highlighting historical events and figures and by appropriating the language and imagery associated with the Spiritual Franciscan tradition. Furthermore, they used a rhetoric of persecution and martyrdom, portraying the Observants as victims of Conventual opposition and emphasizing their resilience in the face of adversity.[269]

Several other relevant aspects are worth noting in these chronicles. They served a polemical purpose, particularly in the ongoing disputes with the Conventuals, justifying the Observance's existence and defending it against accusations of heresy and disobedience. The chronicles also reveal a strong emphasis on public image and reputation, with chroniclers like Oddi highlighting the need for the Observants to project an image of sanctity and moderation.[270] Finally, the chronicles reflect internal tensions within the Observance itself concerning the balance between the eremitical, contemplative ideal of the early movement and the active, preaching-focused approach that emerged under figures like Bernardino of Siena. These tensions are clear in the contrasting portrayals of different *beati* and in the debates over issues like poverty, obedience, and learning.

Chronicles approached these purposes in several ways. Bernardino Aquilano's narrative offers a geographically and thematically limited

---

269   Lappin (2000).
270   Lappin (2000).

perspective on the development of the Observant identity and expansion of the movement within the Franciscan Order during the fourteenth and fiftennth centuries. The chronicle covers a period of a hundred and fifty years, starting from the early attempts at stricter observance of the Franciscan Rule to establishing the Observants as a distinct branch within the Order. The chronicler highlights early reform efforts and the transition from informal groups of reformers to a more organized and officially sanctioned branch within the Franciscan Order. Tensions with the Conventuals, popular piety, miracles, and sanctity make up other central themes of interest for Aquilano who organised the text chronologically, with each chapter focusing on specific events or periods in the development of the Observant movement. As for his sources, rarely does he cite specific documents, such as papal bulls. Instead, he relies on personal observations, eyewitness accounts from other friars, and oral traditions circulating within the Order.

Among the Observant chronicles, Glassberger's work stands out for its comprehensive scope and goal to establish a definitive corpus of information, providing the order with a sense of truthfulness. The author emphasized the Observants' rightful integration within the original Franciscan Order while he differentiated it from other branches. Glassberger surpassed other similar narratives in the ability to demonstrate continuity with the past and highlight the connections between the Observant Franciscans and other religious and political groups. If the awareness of their origins was a concern for other order chronicles as well, few chroniclers showed interest in providing such exhaustive information. With this extensive narrative, Glassberger not only sought to reinforce the Observant identity but also positioned it within the context of the Franciscan Order.

Glassberger's interest in constructing a compelling narrative of Observant history and identity emerges at several levels of his text. The prologue and opening of the chronicle employ rich metaphorical language and superlative terms to portray the Franciscan Order as a divine source of illustrious and saintly figures.[271] Phrases like "clara nomina," "titulos nobiles," and "glorias triumphales" underline ideas of greatness and holiness. Then the image of a "fruitful field infused with heavenly dew" reinforces this notion of divine favor.[272] The chronicle then is presented,

---

271 Glassberger, *Chronicle*, 1-6.
272 Glassberger, *Chronicle*, 1: Illustrium virorum, frater adamate, quos Religionem nostram sacerrimam *veluti agrum frugiferum coelesti infusum rore*, cuique Dominus benedixit in suae institutionis primordiis.

in a manner typical of older chronicles, as an act of avoiding neglect and preserving the Observant Franciscan identity by providing models of holy living for future generations to imitate. In the same section, Glassberger uses further images to portray Saint Francis as the unshakeable foundation (*lapis fundamentalis*) and perfect example (*virum perfectum*) that strengthen his positive approach to the Order's history.[273]

His concern for preserving and promoting a distinct Observant identity within the Franciscan order emerges at other levels as well. Integrated in the chronicle, Capistrano's letter to the community in Leipzig emphasizes the need to differentiate the Observants from the Conventuals, both in their internal practices as well as in terms of external appearances. This insistence on visual differentiation underscores the importance of maintaining a clear boundary between the two branches of the order. Moreover, Capistrano's detailed prescriptions for the novices' spiritual formation, such as regular meditation, confession, and devotional practices, generate a shared set of religious behaviors and experiences that defined Observant identity. By adhering to these practices, the novices were expected to internalize the values and ideals of the Observance, becoming imitators of Saint Francis. Capistrano's opposition to lay persons dining with the friars highlights his intention to maintain a distinct religious identity and authority in the eyes of the laity.[274]

Glassberger also reinforced the sense of a shared Observant identity and mission by reference to internal events. His account of the Order's growing recognition and legitimacy within the Church, supported by papal endorsements, marks a significant moment in Franciscan history. The backing of Pope Honorius III or of other high-ranking officials, as evidenced by the letters of endorsement for the Observants, the General Chapter of 1219, the election of ministers, and the permission granted to friars to preach in Europe and beyond, constituted important steps in the expansion and construction of the Order's identity as a recognized religious community.[275] Furthermore, the narrative reflects the efforts of defending the Observants' way of life, by drawing on canonical and historical precedents to support their case.[276] It is along these lines, that Glassberger presents the Poor Clares of Nuremberg as models of

---

273 Glassberger, *Chronicle*, 3.
274 Glassberger, *Chronicle*, See above, the letter addressed to the community in Leipzig.
275 Glassberger, *Chronicle*, 12-13.
276 Glassberger, *Chronicle*, 353.

reformed religious life, by pointing to the close relationship between them and the Observant Franciscans.[277]

The diverse elements in the portrayal of Observant identity in the chronicles of both Glassberger and Aquilano are connected and reinforced through several narrative strategies: chronological ordering, focus on key figures, anecdotal storytelling, or use of documentary sources. To understand how these strategies combined to shape the principles of the Franciscan Observants, the following analysis will attend to several textual levels. First, I will examine how authorial intentionality prompted the chroniclers to present themselves and their objectives within these narratives. Second, I will look at how significant moments and issues in Franciscan history are depicted to highlight the Observants' growth and challenges. Third, the process of othering of foreign groups like Greeks or Turks shows how interactions with external groups shaped self perception. Lastly, the examination of diverse forms of stories, such as narratives of conflict or biographies, will illustrate the moralizing core of the Observant chronicles as well as the personal examples of Observant virtues. These four textual levels correspond to the dimensions of identity discussed above: the order's efforts of legitimation and its intellectual and educational background.

III.1. Authorial fashioning

An initial step in this analysis is to look at how the authors fashioned themselves and their role in the narrative.[278] If authors continued to rely on narrative traditions or the established authorities, be they Biblical, classical, or ecclesiastical, they become present in the historical narratives of the later Middle Ages.[279] To be sure, their presence was rather discrete, in line with their intention to instill an objective tone to their composition. Chronicle authors drew on modesty *topoi* such as when Glassberger expressed his own lack of skill (*imperitia*) and fear of diminishing the successful deeds of past Franciscans with his "humble and rustic speech.[280]" Even if scarce, conventional, or hidden behind information borrowed from other sources, authorial remarks on the design and goals of the text help us get an insight into how personal and collective identities were accommodated in the Observant identity.

---

277 Glassberger, *Chronicle*, 282.
278 On authorship in medieval chronicles see especially Bratu (2019).
279 Bratu (2019).
280 Glassberger, *Chronicle*, 3.

By constantly displaying raw event material, chronicle authors fashion themselves as standing close to the events recounted and holding an expert knowledge. In the prologue to his chronicle, Aquilano speaks about the approach to the information and the relation with other friars. He justifies his chronicle in a straightforward manner:

> Non sine dolore cordis haec scribo. Novi enim, quod in hac nostra familia sunt plurimi fratres in arte dicendi durissimi, conscientiae eliminatae, qui hoc opus summa cum omnium consolatione scripsissent, idque minime fecerunt; nec mihi notum est, quod aliquis faciat.
>
> I do not write these things without a heavy heart. For I know that in this our family there are many brothers most learned in the art of speaking and refined in conscience, who would have written this work with the utmost consolation for all; and in no way did they do so.[281]

But this standard opening of a chronicle belied institutional ambivalence and conflict. By voicing his reluctance to write the chronicle, Aquilano acknowledged that other learned Observants did not write a chronicle before him, which suggests the lack of prioritization of documenting their history within the order's hierarchy. Later he points out that when he proposed recording miracles and history to the "general chapter," they showed no interest, again proving lack of political will to preserve history within the order's hierarchy. He shows himself compelled to record things for the "consolation and information of posterity," rather than let important events fade into silence because of the leadership's neglect. In this way, Bernardino's polemical language depicts an Observant congregation experiencing tensions, debating over priorities, and lacking authoritative mandate for historical works like his chronicle. His introduction becomes a document asserting authorial autonomy in choosing to narrate their history.

By contrast, Glassberger presents himself in the tradition of other Franciscan teachers. His programmatic preface to the chronicle is written in the form of a letter, a choice that reflects the modes of expression in the *vitae* of John Capistrano as both Nicolaus de Fara and Christopher of Varese also begin with similar dedicatory letters.[282] There, Glassberger indicates a preference for a *concise and simple style* (succincte stiloque simplici)

---

281 Aquilano, *Chronicle*, 1.
282 See Nicolaus de Fara, *AASS* and Christopher of Varese, *AASS*.

intended to emphasize the didactic value of his historical collection and the reliance on previous authoritative sources. He lists his sources or invites his readers to look further into other writings. For instance, when reporting on the death of John Capistrano, he refers to Christopher of Varese, Nicolaus de Fara, and other *socii*, who wrote on Capistrano's life.[283]

As for the treatment of events, given the numerous conflicts and tensions recounted in the chronicles, authors represent themselves as experts and mediators. In Glassberger's case, this strategy appears more explicit than in Aquilano, as he reproduces numerous sources in support of his account which occasionally takes the form of an official report.[284] Still, although he relied on a wealth of additional sources, Glassberger inserted his own voice and views, such as when criticizing lax interpretations of the Rule.[285] These examples suggest that, through direct and indirect self-representation, chroniclers not only documented the history of the Observance but actively shaped the Observant identity as self-styled authoritative custodians of the Franciscan tradition.

III.2. Narrating Franciscan institutional recognition and religious authority

Naturally, in their construction of Observant identity, both chronicles predominantly approached aspects of the Franciscan history and ideals in numerous episodes or allusions. As mentioned, Glassberger details the early stages in the history of the Franciscan Order, with the result that his focus remains for a substantial section of the chronicle on the succession of Franciscan ministers and events in Central Europe:

> Anno Domini 1229 frater Iohannes Angelicus primus visitator in Theutoniam est missus, qui cum omni tranquillitate et pace fratres caritative admonebat et informabat et ad patientiam inducebat. Et eodem anno fratres in Ratisbona de capella Salvatoris solemne monasterium auxilio nobilium de Drucksatz, de Eckenmul et comitum de Pogen construxerunt, et fundum dederunt nobiles de Paulstorff.

> In 1229, Iohannes Angelicus was sent as the first visitor to Germany, who kindly admonished, instructed, and encouraged the brothers with all tranquility and peace, leading them to patience. And in the same year,

---

283 Glassberger, *Chronicle*, 384.
284 E.g. Glassberger, *Chronicle*, 321-323.
285 E.g. on the diregard of the rule of poverty, Glassberger, *Chronicle*, 295 and 261.

the brothers in Regensburg built a monastery with the assistance of the nobles of Drucksatz, Eckenmul, and the counts of Pogen, and the nobles of Paulstorff provided the land.[286]

A close reading of Glassberger's narrative of events reveals the chronicler's strategy to zoom into polemical issues involving early Franciscans. A telling example was the controversy about the secular and religious powers, in which, as discussed, the Franciscans were involved in the political and ideological conflicts opposing the papacy and the Holy Roman Empire. The chronicle echoes how Franciscan scholars like William of Ockham, a prominent Franciscan theologian and philosopher, played a role in defending the idea of monarchy and King Louis in particular against the accusations of heresy put forward by the supporters of a strong papal power.[287] Glassberger introduces Ockham's treatise, *Opus nonaginta dierum* (*The Work of Ninety Days*), which argued for the separation of papal and imperial powers, asserting that both derive their authority directly from God but have distinct spheres of influence - the papal power in spiritual matters and the imperial power in temporal matters. As mentioned, Ockham's arguments challenged the notion of papal supremacy and the idea that the Pope had universal jurisdiction and absolute power in temporal affairs. Gassberger thus appears to align with Ockham's defense of the imperial cause in relation to the papacy, blurring the lines between their spiritual ideals and political allegiances.

The interest in the political ideas pertaining to defining authority becomes evident when the chronicler considers King Louis' stance on the issue.[288] Glassberger reconstructs Louis' assertion of his authority and defense of the legitimacy of his rule against claims that it might derive from the Pope. The author appears to agree with the king's refutation of arguments that the Pope's authority supersedes the monarchical one, citing legal and theological reasoning to support separating temporal and spiritual powers. Eventually, he affirms the divine origin of his authority which, he argues, was not dependent on papal anointing, consecration, and coronation. In support of this position, Glassberger mentions that King Louis cited decrees, which emphasized the distinct roles and jurisdictions of the papal and imperial powers, stating that neither should usurp the rights of the other. With the details of this controversy, Glassberger

---

286 Glassberger, *Chronicle*, 48.
287 Glassberger, *Chronicle*, 297.
288 Glassberger, *Chronicle*, 171.

highlighted the Franciscan efforts to balance religious principles with the complex political and social dynamics of medieval Europe.

But the controversy was not only theoretical, as the chronicle illustrates the conflict with other concrete examples of clashes between Franciscan ideals and political realities. Following the same strategy of integrating the Franciscans into institutional structures, Glassberger includes episodes pointing to the early growing recognition and acceptance of the Franciscan Order by the Church hierarchy. For instance, the chronicle recounts the endorsement of Cardinal Hugolino and Pope Honorius III as a turning point in the Order's history, legitimizing its existence and mission and connecting it with the long history of the Franciscans.[289] This appointment, Glassberger suggests, provided the Order a solid position within the Church hierarchy and secured its future growth and development. Further anchoring the Franciscans within institutional history, Glassberger portrays Saint Francis through familiar hagiographical tropes, like childhood piety, renunciation of wealth, and embrace of poverty, resonating with his Observant audience.[290]

This historical grounding together with the institutional recognition from the Church hierarchy, as highlighted by Glassberger, positioned the Franciscans as players in the ecclesiastical landscape, enabling their involvement in reform efforts and the fight against heresies, as evidenced by the chronicle's detailed accounts of Church councils and decrees. The papacy played a significant role in promoting the Rule through declarations and official pronouncements. This intervention, while aiming to provide clarity and unity, sparked tensions with other Franciscans who sought greater autonomy in defining their own way of life. The chronicler often adopts the voice of the ecclesiastical authorities.[291] This occurs especially in the narratives dedicated to the events occurring in the first half of the fifteenth century, as for instance, when he includes a decree issued by the Council of Basel in response to a petition from the Abbess Margaret and the convent of the monastery of Poor Clares in Alspach, in the diocese of Basel. According to the document, the nuns had been reformed and brought back to regular observance with the help from the Franciscan Order. Their request was to continue under the guidance of a virtuous Franciscan who could lead them by his example. The Council granted the Custos (guardian) of the Franciscans in the Province of Strasbourg, Nicholas Caroli, and his

---

289 Glassberger, *Chronicle*, 12.
290 Glassberger, *Chronicle*, 4-6.
291 Glassberger, *Chronicle*, 258-260.

successors, the power to appoint a confessor and suitable friars to assist the nuns, as well as to visit, inquire, correct, and reform the monastery in accordance with the constitutions and institutes of the Franciscan and Poor Clare Orders.[292]

In the other chronicle, Aquilano depicts the Franciscans' relations to secular and ecclesiastical leaders as less prominent for the order's evolution than in Glassberger's account. He presents the Franciscans engaged with local authorities, seeking their protection. The narrative describes how they gained the favour of the people and rulers of Perugia, which helped them establish their presence in the city. Such pragmatism suggests a calculated willingness to work within existing local power structures to advance their cause.[293] Instead, Aquilano portrays the Franciscans as seeking and relying upon papal support for their movement. He offered special attention to Popes Martin V, Eugene IV, and Calixtus III for approval, protection, and formal recognition.[294] This suggests that, more than Glassberger, Aquilano promoted a stronger belief in the authority of the papacy and its role in resolving internal disputes and guiding religious practice.

The chronicles do not focus only on external events but also on events in the affairs of the order like the transition of leadership, from Saint Francis to his immediate successors or the growth of the order. Aquilano's account channels the readers' attention to internal dynamics of the Observant expansion. He highlights the image of Paulutius of Foligno as a key figure in formalising the Observant way of life within the Order. Aquilano credits Paulutius with initiating the "observance of the family in the Order.[295]" Establishing a vicar general for Observant friars, the ability to hold their own general congregations, and the granting of authority to elect their own vicars and guardians indicate the recognition and acceptance of the Observants as a distinct branch within the Franciscan Order. But while he mentions the Observants' presence in Catalonia, Dalmatia, Corsica, Sicily, Sardinia, Bohemia, Austria, or Poland, he does not record the precise details about the order and the timing of specific foundations.[296] This suggests that, in his view, the expansion was driven by local circumstances, opportunities, and the availability of committed individuals, rather than a centrally coordinated plan.

---

292 Glassberger, *Chronicle*, 310-312.
293 Aquilano, *Chronicle*, 11.
294 E.g. Aquilano, *Chronicle*, 26-29.
295 Aquilano, *Chronicle*, 6-7.
296 Aquilano, *Chronicle*, 75-79.

On the other hand, Glassberger is more systematic in his consideration of the challenges faced by the Franciscans in their growth. He recounts the episodes associated with Francis' declining health and the impact of his follower's, Peter, miracles on the community's way of life.[297] Later, the chronicle presents the challenges faced by the Franciscans as they expanded into new territories, challenges that involved not only efforts but also miraculous solutions. For instance, Glassberger narrates an episode involving a group of Observants traveling from Trent to Lindau. Upon their arrival, two of them visited the castle of Michelsteyn, where the local ruler, despite preparing a battle, treated them well. After dinner, the lady of the castle asked them to pray for her husband's safety and assured by one brother through divine guidance, they prayed for peace. Miraculously, one adversary proposed peace, which was agreed upon by the lord of place. This event fostered a deep devotion from the lord towards the Franciscans. Years later, the daughter of the ruler had Fredebald as her confessor. Upon his death, her son fell ill but, in desperation, she sought divine intervention by tying relics of Fredebald around her son's neck. Through prayer and divine intervention, her son was healed. The son, previously bold and warlike, later joined the monastic ranks after these miraculous events, which were recounted after Saint Francis's death.[298]

The story illustrates how miracles punctuated Glassberger's narrative of the growth of the Franciscan order and eventually the construction of its identity. Many chronicle stories hold miraculous elements underscoring the divine favor and spiritual significance attributed to the events they describe. In one such episode, the chronicler narrates the miracle which Saint Francis performed in the presence of a certain Bartholomaeus, a man who had a demon in his house. When Francis approached, the demon fell silent for three days until the saint departed. Bartholomaeus then questioned the demon who revealed that Francis was recognized as a significant figure by both demons and heaven, and that he would lead many to repentance and holiness.[299] Such miracles surface with a high frequency. Even the moment of Saint Francis' death prompts Glassberger to deal with the miracles legitimizing his legacy. After Francis passed away, people witnessed miraculous signs on his body, such as the wounds of Christ, which many kissed and touched. Despite his wish to be buried in Saint Mary of the Portiuncula Church, fear of his body being taken by

---

297 Glassberger, *Chronicle*, 32.
298 Glassberger, *Chronicle*, 36-37.
299 Glassberger, *Chronicle*, 25-26.

the people of Perugia led the citizens of Assisi to bury him in the church of Saint George, where he had learned and preached as a boy.[300]

If Glassberger wove miracles into his narrative, Aquilano adopted a nuanced and critical approach to reporting miraculous events, reflecting a methodology that distinguishes his work within the context of fifteenth-century hagiography. His attention to detail is evident in his explicit standards for verification, cautious use of language, hierarchical evaluation of miracle types, attention to contextual frameworks, selective reporting practices, critical analysis of accounts, and pragmatic application of narratives towards specific aims.

A cornerstone of Bernardino's approach was his rigorous standard for verification, as seen in his strict differentiation between personal observation and hearsay. For example, when describing an event related to Saint Bernardinus, he states *Et quando in die Assumptionis Dominae nostrae praedicavit…et stella quaedam in acre apparuit…et ego vidi*,[301] thereby establishing the veracity of the account through direct eyewitness testimony. Furthermore, he attributes the sources of his accounts, as in his reporting on John Capistrano:

> Socii tamen ejus, quos ego sibi de nostra provincia miseram ad partes istas, multa miracula scripta retulerunt, quae per viros a domino illius terrae constitutos ad hoc examinata et scripta fuerunt.
>
> However, his companions, whom I had sent to him from our province to those parts, brought back many written miracles, which were examined and written down by men appointed for this purpose by the lord of that land.[302]

Aquilano's language further reflects his critical stance. He frequently employs qualifiers such as "ut aiunt fratres" or "ferunt," indicating an awareness of the limitations inherent in second-hand accounts and the need for further verification. This caution is further exemplified by his explicit acknowledgment of gaps in his knowledge. Regarding Hieronymus, he expresses his ignorance about any of his miracles ("Huius nullum novi

---

300 Glassberger, *Chronicle*, 43.
301 Aquilano, *Chronicle*, ch. 6.
302 Aquilano, *Chronicle*, ch. 24.

miraculum ") demonstrating a willingness to admit the limits of his information rather than embellishing or fabricating details.[303]

Bernardino's reporting reveals a hierarchical evaluation of miracles, prioritizing evidence based on the nature of the event. He differentiates between the "vita mirabilis," or the virtuous life of an individual, healing miracles, and supernatural phenomena. Notably, he shows a preference for documenting virtuous living over sensational miracles, aligning with the Observant emphasis on moral rectitude. Moreover, he applies strict veracity standards to extraordinary claims, as evidenced by the detailed documentation of the miracles attributed to Bernardino of Siena during his canonization process.[304] This hierarchical approach highlights a discerning perspective that values the quality and reliability of evidence over the sheer quantity or spectacular nature of miraculous accounts. He places miracle accounts within specific historical contexts, linking them to documented events and named witnesses. For instance, the healings are situated within specific times and places, with named individuals corroborating the event.[305] This contextualization lends credibility to the accounts by grounding them in verifiable historical realities.

Bernardino's practices of selective reporting further underscore his critical approach. He chooses to report miracles that underpin the Observant reform, are confirmed by reliable witnesses, and exemplify specific virtues promoted by the movement. This selectivity is evident in his focus on miracles demonstrating Observant values. He explicitly states when he omits miracle accounts, as in his statement, "De aliis vero sanctis viris...nihil aliud dicam,[306]" suggesting a deliberate editorial decision to include only the most pertinent and well-grounded narratives. Beyond reporting of miracles, Bernardino engages in critical analysis, sometimes offering natural explanations alongside supernatural ones. This proves an awareness of alternative interpretations as seen in his detailed account of examining resurrection miracles for Saint Bernardino's canonization.[307] In this way, he keeps the focus of his narrative on the practical implications of miracles among the Franciscans, emphasizing moral lessons over supernatural spectacle.

---

303   Aquilano, *Chronicle*,
304   Aquilano, *Chronicle*, ch. 11.
305   For instance, Aquilano records the case of the resurrection of dead individuals, Aquilano, *Chronicle*, 36.
306   Aquilano, *Chronicle*, ch. 6: "Concerning the other holy men...I will say nothing else".
307   Aquilano, *Cronicle*, ch. 11, 35-38.

III.3. The Observants as viewed in the chronicles

Even if the early trajectory of the Franciscan Order plays a large part, the chronicles' focus remains on the episodes illustrating the ideals and the challenges of the Observance. To a large extent, these episodes reflect the issues present in the Franciscan general history. Like with the Franciscan history, both Aquilano and Glassberger construct the image of a rapid growth of the Observant congregation, suggesting on numerous occasions that even a small number of friars residing in a particular place were perceived as a force of change that warranted the attention of power brokers like local leaders, kings, or nobles.

At the core of Glassberger's work lies the pursuit of the ideals of poverty and obedience in parallel with the configuration of an institutional identity of the Observance. His chronicle abounds in debates over interpreting these ideals in the Rule and the corresponding papal declarations, reflecting the fragmented nature of the Franciscan order during this period. This focus finds instantiations in several episodes like the events he recounts for the year 1456. On this occasion, he details Pope Pius II's decree against appeals to future councils, a move aimed at centralizing papal authority. By including this episode, Glassberger aligns the Observants with papal power, presents them as guardians of true faith in turbulent times, and also offers a way to differentiate them from other Franciscan groups. Glassberger advances arguments for their legitimacy not through spiritual lineage, but through political allegiance and obedience to Pope Pius II, portrayed as the true shepherd and Vicar of Christ.[308] The Observants' institutional identity emerges in other moments as well, like in the accounts about the geographical extension of the Franciscan order. The portrayal of Dithmarus, a monk traveling to the Holy Land and reporting back to the Pope about its condition hints at the growing interest in the region and the potential for future Franciscan missions there.[309]

It is in this process of consolidating an institutional identity that Glassberger presents the reasons he recounts the early Observant missions in German lands and relates episodes detailing the difficulties but also the opportunities encountered by the friars. The presence of the order in the Upper Rhine region in 1426, allows him to focus on the expansion and reform of the Heidelberg friary.[310] Mechthilde, wife of Count Palatine Ludwig III, who had observed the strict religious life of the Observants in

---

308 Glassberger, *Chronicle*, 363-364.
309 Glassberger, *Chronicle*, 12.
310 Glassberger, *Chronicle*, 282-286.

her home region and desired to have them introduced in Heidelberg to replace the lax Conventual friars, initiated the reform. At first, there was resistance and instability, as the Provincial Minister Jodocus transferred friars between Heidelberg and other friaries like Rufach, impeding the progress of the reform. But the French Observants brought in by Mechthilde would return home when they saw the lack of stability. A key figure in this episode was Nicolaus, a priest who, according to the chronicle, had a divine revelation to join the Franciscans and promote the Observance. As guardian in Heidelberg, he intended to leave with the French friars due to the instability, but Mechthilde convinced him to stay. She, Glassberger narrates, convinced her husband, Ludwig, to write to the Vicar of the Touraine province to send enough Observant friars that the Provincial Minister could not remove or disperse. Because of their strict way of life, the Observants who arrived in Heidelberg attracted recruits from the university students there. Their reputation for holiness spread and inspired other rulers to reform the friaries in their territories as well.[311] Thus, by introducing the Observance and the reform of the Heidelberg friary under the patronage of Mechtilde of Savoy, Glassberger illustrated the role played by secular rulers promote the Observant cause. Despite the challenges, the spread of the reform to other friaries under the patronage of various princes shows the chroniclers' insistence with the growing appeal and influence of the Observant movement.

But however positive many episodes may have been, Aquilano and Glassberger's chronicles also point to the potential for divisions and spiritual crisis within the Order. Aquilano was preoccupied with the challenges to Observant leadership and authority. He mentions a "great discord" during Bernardino of Siena's time as Vicar General of the Observants in Italy.[312] This discord involved tensions between the Vicar of the province and other friars, suggesting disagreements over leadership styles and decision-making processes. In the lead-up to the 1451 general chapter in Perugia, Aquilano notes that Friars Robert of Lecce and John of Volterra felt they had not received "due honour".[313] Other episodes echo similar concerns about neglect, negative examples, or harsh corrections especially by the Ministers.

As for Glassberger, his chronicle includes several stories of disturbance caused by the influx of visitors to convents and the overabundance of

---

311 Glassberger, *Chronicle*, 282-286.
312 Aquilano, *Chronicle*, 24-25.
313 Aquilano, *Chronicle*, 39-40.

offerings during celebrations of miracles, a situation which illustrated the challenges faced by the Observants in maintaining their commitment to poverty and simplicity in the face of growing popularity and institutional growth.[314] Still, despite occasional dissensions and issues, the chronicles used these stories especially for exemplifying the Observants' role as peacemakers and spiritual advisors.[315]

As already suggested, chronicles promoted the Observant identity not only through examples of cooperation or dissension but also through moralization and institutionalization of communities. In Glassberger's chronicle, a letter by Bernardino of Siena who addressed the Italian friars emphasized the moderate use of material goods, the necessity for distinguishing superfluity and curiosity, and the adherence to the judgments of superiors in doubtful matters.[316] The chronicles' insistence on conformity to these declarations and on the threat of excommunication and imprisonment, underscored the importance of a shared understanding and practice of the Franciscan Rule for the coherence and unity of the Observant movement.[317]

Another decree presented in the chronicle reflects the Observants' emphasis on bringing religious communities back to regular observance and discipline. The nuns of Alspach have been "salubriter reductae" (healthily brought back) to the norm of discipline and observance of the Poor Clares by the efforts of some devout Franciscan friars. The Council commended this "salutiferum reductionis et reformationis opus" (salutary work of reduction and reformation) and expressed its desire that the nuns continue to make progress in this discipline.[318] Similarly, the Observant reforming identity emerges from Cardinal Nicholas of Cusa's efforts to help the Poor Clare monastery in Brixen using his apostolic authority. That he had to seek sisters from the Province of Strasbourg because of the lack of reformed monasteries in the Province of Austria underscored the need for reform and the importance of the Observant movement in promoting regular observance.[319]

The chronicle also cites the decrees issued at the Council of Constance, which allowed the Observants to govern themselves under an elected vicar. This decree was approved by Pope Martin V and confirmed by the

---

314 Glassberger, *Chronicle*, 32.
315 Glassberger, *Chronicle*, 36-37.
316 Glassberger, *Chronicle*, 302-305.
317 Glassberger, *Chronicle*, 302-305.
318 Glassberger, *Chronicle*, 310-312.
319 Glassberger, *Chronicle*, 353.

Council of Basel and Pope Eugene IV, who expanded and instituted the document under which the Observants lived. John Capistrano argued that the Observants could not be forced to abandon these decrees and questioned what the Christians would think if they saw the poor servants of Christ, who intend to fulfill their vows to God, as they were persecuted by those who should protect them.[320]

The chronicles' extensive documentation of papal decrees, council decisions, and regulatory frameworks reveals more than administrative concerns. It shows how the Observants understood and constructed their identity through institutionalizing the Observant identity within the Franciscan Order and the Church at large. Recording papal bulls, council decisions, and internal pronouncements served not merely as historical documentation, but as a strategy to solidify the Observants' position within the broader Franciscan order and the Church itself. By emphasizing adherence to regulations, the chronicles constructed a narrative of the Observants as a group committed to discipline and the proper interpretation of Franciscan ideals. The emphasis on institutional authority provided a framework for resolving internal disputes, dealing with intricate local politics, and, ensuring the growth and stability of the Observant movement. The chronicles, therefore, offer arguments for their legitimacy and authority rooted in a demonstrable commitment to established rules and the decrees of both ecclesiastical and secular powers. This strategic alternation of the legal and institutional frameworks distinguished the Observant chronicles from other communication tools like sermons or hagiography, by revealing their concern with not just the spiritual, but also the political and social dimensions of their movement's survival and success.

III.4. Ideals in the formation of Observant identity: from spiritual models to political power

In parallel to the emphasis on the institutional frameworks and regulatory authority, the Observant chronicles balanced the concern for legal regulations with spiritual formation. This dual emphasis becomes evident in their treatment of ideals and distinctive characteristics that shaped Observant identity, where they portrayed the movement not as innovative but as restoring Francis's original vision. Their identity remained anchored in the Franciscan Rule, which served as a divinely sanctioned blueprint for their way of life. The chronicles provide a panorama of virtues that reflect both the Franciscan ideal and the intellectual and ethical landscape

---

[320] Glassberger, *Chronicle*, 355.

of the late Middle Ages. These virtues transcend mere personal qualities, extending into the communal and institutional values that defined the Observant Franciscan movement.

In particular, Glassberger portrayed Saint Francis' divine reception of the Rule, emphasizing its spiritual authority and the need of faithful adherence. It was the reason Glassberger presented a vivid narrative of the events surrounding the confirmation of the Franciscan Rule, including Francis' retreat, the divine revelation of the Rule, and the miraculous appearance of the stigmata.[321] Francis' last days also served to illustrate moral ideals. The chronicle details his physical suffering and the relinquishment of his leadership role because of infirmities, culminating in the appointment of his successor, Peter Cattani.[322] Francis entrusted the care of the Order to Peter and submitted to the authority of the Ministers. Despite being missed by the others, Glassberger notes that Francis accepted his diminished role until his death. Peter, renowned for his miracles, was buried with great honor; however, Francis, concerned about the attention his tomb received, commanded him to cease performing miracles even in death. This extensive account of Francis and Peter serves not merely to honor the founder of the Order, but also to emphasize obedience among the Observants.

Beside the attention for the roots of the order, the chronicles focused on individual features of the Observant identity. Glassberger introduced stories to illustrate the virtues of charity. For instance, the narrative of the daughter of the King of Hungary, Elizabeth's acts exemplifies the Observants' emphasis on humility and mercy, reinforcing their image as compassionate spiritual leaders dedicated to serving the poor and the marginalized.[323] In his turn, Aquilano portrays poverty and austerity not as rules to be followed, but as active expressions of faith and identity commitment. He describes the early Observant friars engaging in practices like walking barefoot and wearing iron sandals, mirroring the poverty of the local populace and embodying the humility of Christ.[324] Aquilano also recounts how Observants, when requesting alms, would stand with *arms outstretched in the form of a cross*, thus pointing to their willingness to embrace suffering.[325] In addition to poverty, Aquilano presents preaching and pastoral care as integral to the Observants' understanding of their

---

[321] Glassberger, *Chronicle*, 36.
[322] Glassberger, *Chronicle*, 32
[323] Glassberger, *Chronicle*, 33
[324] Aquilano, *Chronicle*, 8-9.
[325] Aquilano, *Chronicle*, 9.

religious identity. He details how Observants, despite initial opposition and persecution, gained widespread popularity and influence through compelling sermons and compassionate engagement with the laity. The account of Paulutius and his companions settling in a remote location, attracting people through their *sanctity of life, regular observance, and greatest devotion, and especially in the assiduity of prayer*, illustrates the emphasis on spiritual renewal and connecting with the religious needs of the people.[326] Similarly, Aquilano's description of Bernardino of Siena's preaching, which ignited *the fire of the Holy Spirit* in his listeners, revealed the potential of eloquent preaching in turning local communities to following the teachings of Saint Francis.[327]

Other virtues like humility (*humilitas*) were also prominent in the chronicles. Aquilano portrays Observant leaders like Paul of Foligno and Bernardino of Siena as exemplars of this virtue, rejecting pride and ambition in favor of service to God and the community. Mirroring the context of the late Middle Ages, when it was juxtaposed with the sin of pride, humility served the chroniclers as a crucial counterpoint to the perceived arrogance and worldliness of the Conventuals. Obedience (*obedientia*) to the rule of Saint Francis and the Church hierarchy formed another cornerstone of the Observant identity as depicted by Aquilano. The chronicle portrays the Observants as steadfastly obedient to both their superiors and the papacy, even amidst internal and external challenges. In a period marked by ecclesiastical and social upheaval, including the Great Schism and the rise of heretical movements, obedience became a paramount virtue for the chroniclers.

Beside the models intended for the broader population and as an echo of the Franciscans' efforts to connect with the educational discourses of their age, the chronicles cultivated a prominent presence of learning and literati among the Observants. Both Aquilano and Glassberger mention Observants who had knowledge about the sophisticated sources of theology. For instance, when describing the activities of Anthony of Padua, he informs the readers of his study of Dionysus Pseudo-Areopagite and the fact that he combined the ardor of his heart with theological reflection.[328] The emphasis on charitable works and intellectual pursuit argue in favor of the idea that the chronicles sought to portray the Observants as maintaining the balance between practical spirituality and scholarly devotion.

---

326 Aquilano, *Chronicle*, 18-19.
327 Aquilano, *Chronicle*, 19.
328 Glassberger, *Chronicle*, 34.

The chronicles extend the discourse of reform in other directions and incorporate ideas derived from the late medieval political theorists. Aquilano and Glassberger reflect concerns with authority, governance, conflict, unity, reform, and the relationship between virtue and power, which were central to the intellectual and political landscape of the time. Primarily, as we have already seen, themes of medieval political thought found echoes in episodes detailing papal authority and legitimacy through virtue. Hierarchical governance and rule of law through legal structures were reflected by the Observants' adherence to the Rule of Saint Francis and their efforts to secure papal decrees for their reforms. The chronicles also emphasize the Observants' role in promoting unity within the Church and society, reflecting the late medieval ideal of Christian unity in the face of threats like heresy and the Ottoman Empire. At the same time the chronicles address the challenges of division especially the factionalism and the lack of stability within the broader Church (e.g. the Great Schism). Moreover, the chronicles reflect key concepts of medieval political philosophy concerning the definition of power and the role of the individual. The Observants' spiritual and moral virtues become sources of power and influence, enabling them to effect change and garner support from both ecclesiastical and lay communities. This portrayal aligns with the medieval idea, present in the works of Augustine and Aquinas, that true power derives from virtue. Conversely, another central Observant idea, the rejection of wealth and ambition becomes a political theme serving as a critique of worldly power and its inherent corrupting influence, echoing the medieval tradition, found in writers such as John of Salisbury and William of Ockham, of criticizing the misuse of power.[329]

The chronicles also highlight the political role of individual leaders, such as the already mentioned, Bernardino of Siena and John Capistrano, in shaping the Observant movement. This emphasis reflects the medieval focus on the role of the virtuous leader in guiding and inspiring others, a theme readily apparent in mirrors-for-princes literature. The chronicles appear interested in the tension between individual charisma and institutional authority, particularly in cases like Robert of Lecce's career, whose personal ambitions led to conflict within the Observant movement. This tension reflected medieval debates concerning the balance between individual agency and maintaining institutional order.

---

329 Nederman (1996).

III.5. Balancing ideals and pragmatism

The chroniclers' attempt to align ideals with ongoing political themes and historical realities further reverberates in the narration of the obstacles encountered by the Observant reform. Many are set against the backdrop of the Western Schism (1378-1417), a period of crisis that saw multiple claimants vying for papal authority. Aquilano invokes the schism when describing the tumultuous events surrounding the 1443 general chapter in Padua, where tensions between Observants and Conventuals flared into open conflict. He notes that some anticipated the chapter would mirror the chaos of the schism, suggesting that this historical event had become synonymous with division and disruption.[330]

With a similar interest in the schism, Glassberger details the controversy that arose when Adam Payn and John Cuock, representing the Augustinian and Franciscan orders, sought assisting Pope Alexander V, elected during the Council of Pisa in 1409 in an attempt to resolve the tensions by deposing the rival popes.[331] The controversy, Glassberger narrates, revolved around the Pope's decree "Regnans in excelsis," which condemned a series of doctrinal errors. Yet, this document appears to have been met with resistance from some members of the University of Paris, who allegedly imprisoned and deprived Mendicants of their rights, and spread falsehoods about the Bull. The conflict highlighted the tensions between the Mendicant Orders, including the Franciscans, clergy, and academic institutions.[332] This example shows that the institutional instability and the need for reform shaped the Franciscan Observant movement, which sought to return to a strict observance of the Franciscan Rule and an authentic spiritual life.

The political dimension of the documents pertaining to the schism is clear in the order's appeal to papal authority to address their grievances and protect their interests. The documents cited by both Aquilano and Glassberger emphasized the importance of unity among the orders in the face of attacks. This unity was deemed not only a practical necessity but also a means of upholding the "truth of faith" and the legitimacy of Pope John XXIII, who was elected during the Council of Constance (1414-1418) in an attempt to resolve the Western Schism. This account of the schism also presented the Franciscan Observance as part of the general discourse

---

330   Aquilano, *Chronicle*, 23-26.
331   Glassberger, *Chronicle*, 239.
332   Glassberger, *Chronicle*, 239.

of ecclesiastical reform and in search of solutions to confront the political landscape of the time while remaining committed to spiritual renewal.

The chroniclers' interest in the narration of obstacles extends beyond the institutional framework and touches on the administration of smaller communities. In 1455, Cardinal Nicholas of Cusa, Bishop of Brixen, sought to reform the Poor Clare monastery by making use of his apostolic authority. As there was no reformed monastery of this order in the Province of Austria to which the monastery belonged, he sent a request to the Provincial Vicar of the Province of Strasbourg and the Guardian of the Nuremberg convent, Albert Puchelbach, with whom he had become acquainted during a legation. In September of the same year, five Poor Clare sisters from Nuremberg were sent by apostolic mandate to Brixen, with the expenses covered by the Cardinal. This was achieved with the cooperation and help of Nicholas Mussell, a citizen of Nuremberg and the sisters' guardian, and three priests, John Lar, the Provincial Vicar, and a certain Albert. One of these sisters was appointed Abbess, and four years later, she returned to the Nuremberg convent with one companion, at which time a third sister was made Abbess.[333]

These chronicles, therefore, offer more than a mere historical record; they present case studies in the sometimes fragile balance between religious conviction and the exigencies of institutional politics. The Observant movement, as depicted in these episodes, emerges not as a monolithic entity, but as a dynamic group, adjusting its strategies of growth at the same time with the adaptation of their narrative expressions. This nuanced portrayal of reform highlights the sophisticated understanding of the chroniclers, who recognized the link between spiritual renewal and the practical realities of their time.

III.6. Otherness

So far, we have seen the chronicles depicting the Observants as adjusting their spiritual ideals to the practical necessities and circumstances. Several aspects appear to have received particular attention: institutional pragmatism, evident in the accounts of reform efforts of various communities; adaptive leadership, emerging from examples ranging from managing relationships with local authorities to showing practical wisdom in achieving spiritual objectives; balance between maintaining autonomous Observant identity and acknowledging broader Church

---

[333] Glassberger, *Chronicle*, 353.

authority; and finally growth visible in acknowledging both miraculous interventions and careful institutional planning.

Yet, the Observant identity was forged not only in relation to other institutions or its own ideals, but also through a deliberate process of differentiation, particularly in relation to the Conventual branch of the Order. By positioning themselves as the true adherents to Saint Francis's original Rule, especially in terms of the emphasis on poverty and simplicity, the Observants contrasted their practices with what they perceived as the Conventuals' deviation from these foundational principles. This self-definition emerges prominently in Glassberger's chronicle, notably in John Capistrano's papal correspondence, where he articulates the fundamental distinctions between Observant and Conventual interpretations of Franciscan life.[334] Aquilano's chronicle provides a nuanced picture of the ongoing tensions and conflicts between the Observant and Conventual branches of the Franciscan Order. While acknowledging the periods of cooperation and shared goals, his chronicle also reveals many disagreements. One of the major sources of tension, Glassberger pointed out, stemmed from the Conventuals' resistance to the Observants' growing autonomy. The Conventuals, representing the more established and less strict interpretation of the Franciscan Rule, viewed the Observants' push for greater independence as a threat to their authority and influence within the Order. Aquilano describes how early attempts by Observants to secure autonomy, like Angelus of Monte Leone's request to observe the Rule more strictly, were met with distrust and resulted in friars being "divided from each other.[335]"

Alongside the rivalry with the Conventuals, the chronicles show the Observants crystallizing their identity through encounters with other ethnic groups, particularly the Greeks, the Ottoman Turks, and the Tatars. Through missionary works and cross-cultural interactions, the Observants faced theological and cultural differences that shaped their self-perception as propagators of the Franciscan rule. These additional portrayals of the *Other* hold significant nuances that echo two of the main religious and political goals to which the Observants were attached: the unity of the church and the resistance against the Ottoman expansion.

---

334   Glassberger, *Chronicle*, 355.
335   Aquilano, *Chronicle*, 3-6.

III.6.1 The Other: Greeks, Tatars, and Turks

Greeks feature prominently in chronicles at the administrative, inter-religious, and intellectual levels, in positive colors. Bernardino Aquilano mentions Byzantine Greek texts which came to be translated into Latin and circulated in the Observant circles. It was the case of John Climacus' *Ladder of Divine Ascent* translated by Angelus da Clareno and retranslated by Ambroggio Traversari.[336] For his part, Glassberger mentions Greek works like the theological essays of Dionysus Pseudo-Areopagite when introducing the Franciscan theologian, Antony of Padua.[337]

But most references to Greeks pertain to administrative matters. Glassberger mentions them as part of the interest in the Franciscans' contribution to the unity of the Church. He recounts an episode in 1254 when John of Parma was sent to Constantinople with letters for the emperor to conduct negotiations on the union of the churches:

> Eodem anno missus est frater Iohannes de Parma a domino Innocentio IV. ad Iohannem, imperatorem Graecorum, et Manuelem, Patriarcham Constantinopolitanum, ut tractaret cum eis de Graecia Romanae Ecclesiae unienda, cum litteris multae recommendationis, in quibus eum pacis Angelum nominavit. Ubi idem Generalis in hac legatione multum vita et sanctitate aedificavit tam Imperatorem quam suos, quam Clerum et populum universum, et supra dicta unione legatos solemnes et mitti litteras per dictos Imperatorem et Patriarcham domino Papae eum apparatu magno procuravit. Sed illi legitimo impedimento compulsi sunt redire; alii tamen cum aequali solemnitate missi fuerunt, et illud negotium feliciter consummatum fuisset, nisi eodem anno et Papa et Imperator ipse ex hac vita decessissent. Et ideo negotium ulterius non processit.

> In the same year, Brother John of Parma was sent by Lord Innocent IV to John, Emperor of the Greeks, and Manuel, Patriarch of Constantinople, to negotiate with them about uniting Greece with the Roman Church, with letters of high recommendation, in which he called him the Angel of peace. During this legation, the same General greatly edified both the Emperor and his court, as well as the clergy and all the people through his life and holiness, and concerning the above-mentioned union, he arranged for solemn legates to be sent and letters to be written by the

---

336 Aquilano, *Chronicle*, 4.
337 Glassberger, *Chronicle*, 32.

said Emperor and Patriarch to the Lord Pope with great ceremony. But they were compelled to return due to legitimate impediment; however, others were sent with equal solemnity, and that business would have been successfully completed, had not both the Pope and the Emperor himself departed from this life in the same year. And therefore the matter proceeded no further.[338]

Unsurprisingly, the towering figure of Bessarion, a former Byzantine Greek official before the Fall of Constantinople in 1453, appears in many episodes. During the time of Pope Calixt III, Besarion was appointed Cardinal protector of the Franciscans (1458). Glassberger mentions his collaboration with the exiled Patriarchy of Constantinople in Rome and with James of the Marches while also hinting at the letters exchanges between the Observants and Bessarion which showed the latter's involvement in organizing of the crusades.[339]

Positive perspectives on the Greeks surface on several occasions. Aquilano describes the Church Union of Greeks and Latins during the papacy of Eugene IV as a success:

> Eugenius papa quartus nostrae familiae fuit singularis amicus, fautor et auctor. Hujus temporibus fuit schisma, eoque ultra montes creatus fuit alius papa, nomine Felix, qui fuit annullatus justo Dei judicio, quia male ingressus fuit. Hujus temporibus valentissimi homines Graecorum ad Italiam venerunt sponte missi, ut articulos disputarent, quibus ecclesia Graecos haereticos tenet, et praecipue de processione Spiritus Sancti. Tandem per sex menses disputaverunt Florentiae et victos se esse confessi sunt. Et cum redirent in Graeciam et tota ecclesia laetaretur de ipsorum reductione, nihil actum extitit: imo ut aiunt vix mortem disputatores, quia victi erant, evadere potuerant; et ita Graeci in sua haeresi remanere voluerunt et postea a Turcis subjugati sunt.

> Pope Eugene IV was a singular friend, supporter and patron of our family. During his time there was a schism, and another pope named Felix was created beyond the mountains, who was annulled by God's just judgment because he had entered wrongly. During his time, very capable men of the Greeks came to Italy of their own accord, sent to dispute the articles by which the church holds the Greeks to be heretics, especially

---

338 Glassberger, *Chronicle*, 73.
339 Glassberger, *Chronicle*, 398.

concerning the procession of the Holy Spirit. Finally, they disputed for six months in Florence and confessed themselves to be defeated. And when they returned to Greece, while the whole church rejoiced at their return to the fold, nothing came of it: indeed, as they say, the disputants could barely escape death because they had been defeated; and thus the Greeks chose to remain in their heresy and were afterward subjugated by the Turks.[340]

Glassberger's chronicle further elaborates on the Greek contribution to the unity of the church and reflects echoes of the council of Ferrara-Florence and the Byzantine delegation:

Eodem anno Basileense concilium ab Eugenio translatum in sessione XXXI. edidit decretum suspensionis domini Eugenii Papae tam a spiritualibus quam temporalibus administrandis iuribus papatus, quod diceret eum contumacem et Ecclesiam scandalizantem. Eugenius autem de Bononia ad Ferrariam profectus, venientibus Imperatore Graecorum, Patriarcha Constantinopolitano et Episcopis Graecis, ibidem concilium celebravit. Concilium autem Basileense et post irritationem ab Eugenio factam non desistebat a prosecutione coepti, sed sollicite invitabat Graecos, ut ad se proficiscerentur. Praevaluit tamen auctoritas Eugenii cum suasionibus plurimorum, ut Graeci Ferrariam accederent, unionem cum Ecclesia facturi. Disputatum fuit ergo de articulis cum Graecis, sed nihil perfectum est propter schisma- subortum.

In the same year, the Council of Basel, transferred by Eugene in its 31st session, issued a decree suspending Lord Pope Eugene from administering both spiritual and temporal rights of the papacy, claiming he was contumacious and scandalizing the Church. However, Eugene, having departed from Bologna to Ferrara, with the arrival of the Emperor of the Greeks, the Patriarch of Constantinople, and the Greek Bishops, celebrated a council there. But the Council of Basel, even after the invalidation made by Eugene, did not desist from pursuing what it had begun, but eagerly invited the Greeks to come to them. However, Eugene's authority prevailed, along with the persuasions of many, so that

---

340   Aquilano, *Chronicle*, 29.

the Greeks went to Ferrara to make union with the Church. Therefore, the articles were disputed with the Greeks, but nothing was accomplished because of the schism that had arisen.[341]

When evoking the role of the Observants in the conflict with the Ottomans, Aquilano recounts the activities of Bartholomaeus de Jano who resided several years in the still Byzantine Constantinople with a mission to get help from the patriarch against the Turcs and work towards the unity of the church:

> Contra conscientiam facerem, si venerabilem patrem fratrem Bartholomaeum de Jano de praedicta provincia silentio praterirem. Hic sancti Bernardini socius fuit et acceptissimus praedicator; hic accessit in Graeciam et per duodecim annos in civitate Constantinopolitana moram traxit, prout ipse mihi retulit. Hic videns, quod civitas praedicta ad manus Turcarum, nisi juvarentur, veniret, Romam perrexit et summo pontifici dixit: "Beatissime Pater! Civitas Constantinopolitana perditur sine fallo, nisi juvetur." Demum civitas illa non adjuta fuit, et ipse paulo post obiit, et civitas illa ante annum elapsum perdita fuit. Videtur, quod divina providentia sibi vitam servaverit, donec inspiratus a Deo summo pontifici nuntiaret. Ex cuius perditione innumera mala christianis subsecuta sunt.

> I would act against my conscience if I passed over in silence the venerable father Brother Bartholomew of Jano from the aforementioned province. He was a companion of Saint Bernardine and a most welcome preacher; he went to Greece and spent twelve years in the city of Constantinople, as he himself told me. Seeing that this city would fall into the hands of the Turks unless helped, he went to Rome and said to the Supreme Pontiff: "Most Blessed Father! The city of Constantinople will be lost without fail unless it receives help." Finally, that city was not helped, and he died shortly after, and that city was lost before a year had elapsed. It seems that divine providence preserved his life until, inspired by God, he could announce this to the Supreme Pontiff. From its loss, countless evils have followed for Christians.[342]

In contrast to their favorable view of the Greeks, the Observants characterized the Ottoman and Tatar presence as a fundamental threat to both their

---

341 Glassberger, *Chronicle,* 300.
342 Aquilano, *Chronicle,* 17.

spiritual mission and territorial integrity of Christian lands. Following the Ottoman expansion into Europe in the mid-fourteenth century, contemporary Franciscan writings, including chronicles, sermons, and letters, reflect mounting anxiety over their relentless advance.[343] By the mid-fifteenth century, what had once been a distant concern had transformed into an immediate crisis as Ottoman forces approached the European heartland. In response, Observant chroniclers cultivated a narrative of Christian resilience, representing their order as a bulwark against this existential threat.

Yet, among the Franciscans in general and the chroniclers in particular the representation of the relations to non-Christian peoples knew several variations. Previously, the Franciscan friars John of Piano Carpini and William of Rubruck, for example, provided contrasting perspectives on the Mongols. Carpini, focused on the military threat, depicted the Mongols as barbaric and the Latin captives among them as having lost their faith because of the extreme conditions of enslavement. He emphasized the need for a strong and unified Christendom to resist the Tatar menace. Rubruck, on the other hand, while acknowledging the brutality of Tatar rule, was more concerned with the pastoral care of Christians in the Tatar camps and attempted conversions. He observed the complex religious landscape and the syncretic practices that had developed, recognizing that even amid enslavement, some Latin Christians kept a sense of their identity, albeit changed by their circumstances. He also noted the difficulty of maintaining a distinct Christian identity without priests and access to sacraments, highlighting the fragility of faith in such a diverse environment.[344]

Building on these initial contacts, chroniclers like Aquilano emphasized the need for prudent governance in the shifting geopolitical tides of the Eastern Mediterranean and implied that Oriental Christians needed administration and regulations against the growing threats.[345] Glassberger documented numerous cases of Franciscans serving Christians amid Islamic domination in the Holy Land and detailed miraculous encounters with Muslim Arabs or Tatars. He portrayed indigenous peoples in positive terms as politically more flexible and as objects of hopeful baptismal mission. In 1341, he narrates, at the request of the successful *Tatar Emperor Ganzi*, Pope Benedict sent two envoys from the Franciscan Order, Nicolaus Boneti, a master of sacred theology, and John, originally from Florence, to preach the Catholic faith to him and his people. And whereas Boneti

---

343   Bisaha (2004).
344   Power (2015).
345   Aquilano, *Chronicle*, 45.

returned to the Curia, John completed the mission among the Tatars with the help of his fellow companions.[346]

The chronicles also recount how another Tatar ruler held the Franciscans in such high esteem that he regarded a certain Francis from Alexandria as his father. The ruler entrusted him with his own son for nurturing and baptizing, as Francis had miraculously cured him of a fistula. Yet, Glassberger continues, after his death, another *Saracen* leader took power and captured the Franciscans gathered at the convent in the city of Amalek, including Francis. They were tortured and finally beheaded, an event which, rather than pointing to the cruelty of the Tatars, was meant to reveal the Franciscans' bravery:

> Anno Domini 1333 reversus est frater Iolianncs de Florentia , nuntius Sedis Apostolicae ad Imperatorem Tartarorum olim missus a domino Papa Benedicto XII , de eadem legatione sua cum litteris magni Khanis et muneribus, portans etiam in certitudinem suae legationis quandarn Bullam, quam cuidam antecessorum eiusdem Imperatoris quondam Clemens Papa IV. miserat. In dictis autem litteris concedebat ipse Imperator domino Papae dominium super omnes Christianos imperii sui, cuiuscumque sectae essent, qui erant innumerabiles, rogando eum, ut praedicatores mitteret ad populum suum convertendum. Qui cum ad dominum Papam Innocentium VI. Avenionem venisset, fuit bene ab eo receptus et auditus; facta vero relatione suae legationis, scripsit dominus Papa capitulo generali, proximo Assisii celebrando, ut ordinaret fratres idoneos ad mittendum, de quibus ipse aliquos Episcopos ordinare vellet. Sed tepescentibus lunc qui negotium debebant promovere, ulterius modicum est processum.

> In the year of Our Lord 1353, Brother John of Florence returned as the Apostolic See's envoy to the Tartar Emperor, originally sent by Lord Pope Benedict XII, carrying letters from the great Khan and gifts, also bringing a Bull to confirm his mission, previously sent by Pope Clement IV to one of the Emperor's predecessors. In these letters, the Emperor granted the Pope dominion over all Christians in his empire, regardless of sect,

---

[346] Glassberger, *Chronicle*, 177: Eodem anno misit rex Tartarorum, nomine Ganzi, honorabiles nuntios ad Papam Benedictum, petens, sibi viros mitti Religiosos in Lege divina ad plenum eruditos pro salutifera gentis suae conversione, et ipse Imperator baptizatus est per Fratres Minores. *In the same year, the Tartar king, named Ganzi, sent honorable messengers to Pope Benedict, requesting that men fully versed in divine law be sent to him for the salvation of his people's conversion, and the Emperor himself was baptized by the Franciscan Friars.*

who were countless, and requested that he send preachers to convert his people. When he arrived in Avignon to see Pope Innocent VI, he was warmly received and listened to. After recounting his mission, the Pope wrote to the upcoming general chapter to appoint suitable friars for the mission, some of whom he himself wanted to ordain as bishops. However, as those who were supposed to advance the matter grew indifferent, little further progress was made.[347]

As for the Ottomans, their image did not hold many nuances for chronicles represented them as an army of merciless enemies, highly destructive and a threat to Christianity to its core. This view was reinforced by practices such as *devshirme*, where young children were taken from conquered territories, the absolute power of the sultan, the destructive raids of *akinji* parties, and the use of pressures to induce surrender.[348] Gradually they regarded the Ottomans as a far more dangerous threat than the heresies affecting other provinces. In line with the general views of the time, chroniclers argued that the Turks "provided nothing" to imitate or emulate and promoted the theme of the bloodthirsty Oriental savages. Aquilano reproduces the letter of the same Bartholomaeus de Jano[349] in which he described the Turks while he lived in Constantinople and deplored the use of *devshirme*.[350]

However fitting for the Franciscan context this negative image of the Ottoman Turks might seem, it was far from uniform among the Christians in contact with the Ottomans. Already in the early fifteenth century, the other major group of Christians of the continent, the Byzantine Orthodox adopted a peaceful and conciliatory attitude towards the Ottomans as reflected in the intense negotiations which occasionally brought Turks and Byzantines together.[351] Prominent clerics and Franciscans like Bessarion and Capistrano showed a completely opposite approach and initiated intense calls for crusading campaigns. Chroniclers, influenced by Capistrano's perspective, portrayed the Turks in a consistently negative light, emphasizing their role as an existential threat to Christianity:

---

347   Glassberger, *Chronicle*, 187.
348   Housley (2012).
349   Mentioned by Aquilano, *Chronicle*, 17.
350   Özcan (2013).
351   Nicol (1994).

Quis enim narrare posset tribulationes, quas passa est christianitas novissimis istis temporibus? pestes, fames, angustias, guerras inter Christianos, occisiones, terrarum destructiones. Quis quaeso sine lacrimarum effusione recolere vel narrare potest, quanta mala fecerit Machometus maledictus Turcus ecclesiae Dei? quot et quantas terras, patrias et provincias christianorum- violenter obtinuit? quis narrare posset, quot milia christiauorum vendidit et quotidie vendit? et utinam non sit-venditurus in posterum! Quotidie contra Christianos lucratur, et quod deterius est omnibus: ubi Christiani per flagella continua emendari deberent, ibi continuo deteriores efficiuntur, ita quod propter eorum malam vitam Turcum ad ipsorum destructionem vocare videntur.

For who could tell of the tribulations that Christianity has suffered in these most recent times? Plagues, famines, hardships, wars among Christians, killings, destruction of lands. Who, I ask, can recall or narrate without shedding tears what great evils the accursed Turkish Mahomet has done to God's church? How many and how great lands, homelands, and provinces of Christians has he violently seized? Who could tell how many thousands of Christians he has sold and sells daily? And would that he might not sell more in the future! Daily he gains against the Christians, and what is worst of all: where Christians ought to be reformed through continuous scourging, there they continually become worse, such that through their evil life they seem to call the Turk to their own destruction.[352]

Along these lines, Aquilano depicts the gathering of the crusaders against the Ottomans and the military operations:

Audiens pater frater Joannes, quod Turcus magnam praeparationem contra Christianos faciebat, ut terram quandam, quae est in litore Danubii, occuparet, quae est magnum obstaculum Turco et magnum auxilium Christianorum et praecipue regni Ungariae, tanquam leo currens ad praedam contra Turcum se opponere voluit. Et quia multitudinem cruciatorum congregaverat et continuo congregabat, relicta Alamania ad Ungariam perrexit.

Father Brother John, hearing that the Turk was making great preparations against the Christians to occupy a certain land which is on the shore of the Danube, which is a great obstacle to the Turk and a great help

---

352 Aquilano, *Chronicle*, 22.

to Christians, especially to the kingdom of Hungary, wished to oppose the Turk like a lion running to its prey. And because he had gathered and was continuously gathering a multitude of crusaders, he left Germany and proceeded to Hungary.[353]

The image of the Turks thus emerges in the narrative accounts related to John Capistrano's efforts for a crusade around the year 1456, an event which Glassberger documented extensively. The chronicle describes John Capistrano's journey down the Danube towards Belgrade. Initially discouraged by the small number of crusaders, the chronicle mentions, Capistrano received divine encouragement through a miraculous golden-lettered arrow appearing during Mass, promising victory through the power of the cross. Pope Calixtus had given him a red cross, received from the Cardinal of Sant'Angelo, the Apostolic Legate. The narrative describes a providential storm on the Danube that forced Capistrano's three ships to shore, seemingly protecting them from an imminent Turkish naval force that soon occupied the area where they would have been. This divine intervention, as interpreted in the chronicle, saved Capistrano and his followers from falling into Turkish hands, casting the Turks as a formidable military threat and an instrument in a divine plan.[354]

The configuration of ethnic and religious otherness by reference to Greeks, Tatars, and Ottomans served the chroniclers as a tool to expand their political vision beyond local concerns and project a transnational identity for the Observant movement by showing them active in two of the main processes shaping the late Middle Ages: the efforts for church unity and the fight against the rising power of the Ottomans. By portraying the Greeks in positive terms, as fellow Christians engaged in theological dialogue and potential allies against the Ottoman threat, the chroniclers introduced a sense of shared religious and cultural heritage that transcended geographical boundaries. This ecumenical approach, evident in the accounts of Church union efforts and intellectual exchanges, aimed to position the Observants as players in the broader Christian world. Conversely, the depiction of the Ottomans and Tatars as a menacing "other" shaped Observant identity in terms of their role as defenders of Christendom against a common enemy. This strategic use of contrasting portrayals not only revealed the Observants' claim to spiritual authority but also justified their calls for crusades and other interventions in the political landscape of the Eastern Mediterranean.

---

353 Aquilano, *Chronicle*, 78-81.
354 Glassberger, *Chronicle*, 364.

III.7. Narrative strategies in the formation of Observant identity

The centrality of the themes discussed above was echoed in the specific chronicle narratives that redefined and disseminated a distinct variant of Observant identity. This approach relied on narrative strands that integrated selected information, moralizing stories, letters, and private or official documents to address the challenges Observants faced in their path to legitimation. As stated above, they show the Observant writers motivated by several goals. Some of these goals like the promotion of papal authority and the revival of the cult of Saint Francis were obvious. But other goals like formulating an articulated response to contemporary political and religious challenges, promoting local interests, presenting religious personalities as figures relatable to the public, and reflecting the authors' personal involvement in the narrated events, were more subtly integrated into the chronicles. By reimagining the form of historical narrative, these multiple purposes resulted in accounts that functioned as tools for spiritual and institutional reform in support of the Observant cause. It is therefore necessary to take a further step in this analysis and consider the dominant narrative strategies and types which the chronicles used to serve these goals.

In handling these purposes, Aquilano's chronicle takes the traits of a personal account which relies on first-hand experiences and direct witnesses' reports. His narrative deploys an anecdotal style, with personal observations into the historical narratives of the struggles of the Observant movement.[355] He recounts his own interaction with another friar about the perception of the Observants, a personal touch that instills a vivid and engaging dimension into his narrative.[356] More than Glassberger, Bernardino employs his own memories and information transmitted through oral traditions. Tellingly, he initiates many reports with phrases like "Relatum fuit mihi" (*It was related to me*) or "Audivi" (*I heard*), pointing to an unmediated approach to writing monastic history.[357]

Less personal in the approach, Glassberger's chronicle stands out among Observant narratives for its details and comprehensiveness of Franciscan history. His text reflects a constant effort to rewrite other sources about political and Church-related events within the context of Observant historiography. This was not an uncommon practice in his

---

355 E.g. Aquilano, *Chronicle*, 62-70 on the bulls of Calixtus III.
356 Aquilano, *Chronicle*, 49.
357 E.g. Aquilano, *Chronicle*, 53-54.

time, for monastic orders produced their own chronicles.[358] Like other contemporaries, Glassberger rewrote the lives of notable figures such as John Capistrano, adapting and transforming the source material to suit his own purposes and the needs of his audience. Yet, far from a mere process of simplification or re-elaboration, Glassberger's rewriting was not uniform or consistent, but varied according to the type of narrative applied, the source of his information, and his own intentions to promote personalities or ideas.

Glassberger's narrative strategy follows a chronological order in which he treats events or personalities either by a brief reference but more often by considering the consequences of the actions he described. In contrast to Bernardino Aquilano, his narrative deploys specific information about people, places, and events related to early Observant communities in Italy and Central Europe. His attention to the intricacies of events is evident in the accounts of early Franciscan history, especially when he carefully documents the yearly succession of leadership, as shown by his constant mentioning of new ministers and vicars:

> Defuncto autem beato Francisco, Ordinem rexit frater Helias, eius Vicarius, usque ad electionem alterius Generalis Ministri.

> After the death of blessed Francis, Brother Elias, his Vicar, governed the Order until the election of another Minister General.[359]

Such statements, including information about specific leaders or notable figures of the Franciscan movement like Anthony of Padua, reinforced the continuity between the Order's foundation and its present state. It is this detailing that allows him to add a sense of veracity to his account, an approach which he stresses especially when mentioning the sources of his narratives.

Still, Glassberger's chronicle does not always follow a smooth succession of events, a typical feature of Aquilano's narrative, but integrates abrupt shifts in focus. Political events are interwoven with extensive digressions like biographies, accounts of miracles, or moral lessons. The disruptions are usually caused by the forms and techniques which Glassberger employed in the construction of his chronicle. This strategy offered the chronicler the benefit of overcoming the problems of listing events year

---

358 Roest (1997).
359 Glassberger, *Chronicle*, 21: Haec ego ex memorati fratris Balduini scriptis extraxi.

by year by juxtaposing brief and extensive accounts in which he could focus on the main themes of his chronicle, the Franciscan order's growth in general and its expansion beyond Italy in particular.

In other instances, Glassberger extended sections of his narrative with summaries or full texts of documents. Illustrative for his technique of combining stories, biography, documents, and letters is his record of events for the year 1409. Glassberger narrates the events of the Council of Pisa in 1409, which was convened to address the ongoing Western Schism. The schism, which began in 1378, saw multiple claimants to the papacy, each with their own supporters. The Council of Pisa attempted to end the schism by deposing the two rival popes, Gregory XII and Benedict XIII, and electing a new one, Alexander V. However, this only complicated matters, as neither Gregory nor Benedict recognized the council's authority, resulting in three contenders to the papacy. Attended by a large number of high-ranking clergy and representatives of local rulers, this council accused and deposed two of the contenders, Gregory XII and Benedict XIII, for perpetuating the schism. In the end, Peter of Candia, the Archbishop of Milan, was elected as Pope Alexander V.[360]

These events allowed Glassberger to transition from institutional history to Pope Alexander's biography which the chronicler presented in highly laudatory terms on account of his support for the Observants. Born in Venice-held Crete, Alexander entered the Franciscan Order from a young age. The chronicle stresses his expert learning by mentioning that he devoted himself to theological studies in Paris and was known for his learning and sanctity of life. As a Franciscan, Glassberger shows, Pope Alexander embodied the order's ideals of poverty and detachment from worldly possessions. By combining character details such as the emphasis on his generosity and information about his actions against the "usurpers" of the Church, the biography suggests that he both lived up to the Franciscan ideals and demonstrated his commitment to the mission of the Church.[361] Yet, keeping with the interest in the Council of Pisa, after the biography, Glassberger returns to the account of events surrounding the council and highlights the role of religious orders, particularly the Dominicans, in supporting the rival popes and prolonging the schism. Despite the participants' efforts, Glassberger remarks, the schism persisted, as both Gregory XII and Benedict XIII continued to receive help from various factions.

---

360 Stump (2024), 23-25.
361 Glassberger, *Chronicle*, 227-229.

Glassberger's lack of concern in following the strict chronology of events emerges from his indirect comments to this episode, for, apart from the narrative and Pope Alexander's biography, the account of the Council of Pisa includes a satirical letter as if from Satan. The letter is addressed to John Dominici, a Dominican friar and Cardinal of Ragusa, who was a supporter of Gregory XII. Dominici opposed the Council of Pisa and worked to maintain Gregory's claim to the papacy. The letter satirizes Dominici's actions and accuses him of perpetuating the schism for his own benefit. It relies on several literary and rhetorical techniques like satire, allegory, or irony and criticizes John Dominici's actions and the state of the Church during the Western Schism. By presenting the letter as if written by Satan, Glassberger highlights the perceived evil and corruption within the Church, as it allows him to deploy ironic praise for Dominici's "evil deeds," "abominable lies," and "unjust sermons." The letter appears as an elaborated literary document: it uses allegorical figures, such as the "daughters" of Satan (e.g., lust, simony, pride, and avarice), to represent the vices within the Church and further employs various rhetorical devices, like repetition (e.g. "oh, dearest serpent"), hyperbole (e.g., "infinite joy," "infinite multitude of demons"), and sarcasm, to emphasize its points.[362] Glassberger also embeds allusions to biblical figures and events, such as *the hardening of Pharaoh's heart* and mentions of famous Christian figures like Arius, who all underscore the gravity of the situation and the apostasy of those perpetuating the schism.[363]

Such strategies of combining documents, events, and biography, either through a personal perspective or through an approach aiming at comprehensiveness of information, helped Observant chroniclers to shape the narrative of the Order as a means of self-presentation, education, and constructing their regional identity. The opening section in Glassberger's *Chronicle*, a history of the early years of the Franciscan order, demonstrates this triple functionality. First, the passage focuses on the life of Saint Francis of Assisi, the founder of the Franciscan Order. By narrating Francis' spiritual journey, his adherence to the Gospel way of life, and his establishment of the Franciscan Order and the Order of Poor Ladies, Glassberger recovered the order's history and emphasized Francis' personality in shaping the Observant movement. Second, the events, examples, and anecdotes presented throughout the chronicle provide the

---

[362] Glassberger, *Chronicle*, 229-231.
[363] Glassberger, *Chronicle*, 229.

audience with clear-cut models of behavior. Francis' radical conversion, his embracing of poverty, and instructions to his followers on how to live a virtuous life were all intended to inspire and guide the audience. Third, the extensive narrative of Franciscan prior history underpins the Observants' historical and geographical mapping of their experience in relation to regional circumstances. Glassberger's chronicle situates Francis' life and early days of the Franciscan Order within a historical and geographical context dominated by key events such as the Fourth Lateran Council and Francis's attempted missions to the Holy Land. This contextualization reinforces a stronger sense of the Observants' unique identity and their place in the history of the Church.[364]

Ultimately, the various strategies of narration reflect the Observants' use of memorialization and retrospection on their history to express distance from other religious orders. By emphasizing Francis' adherence to the core values of poverty, humility, and obedience but also integrating documents and anecdotal accounts, Glassberger singularized the Observants from other religious orders that may have strayed from these ideals. The temporal distance between Francis' life and the moment of Glassberger's writing becomes a tool to highlight the Observants' identity and their commitment to recovering the Franciscan way of life.

III.7.1. Types of chronicle narratives

These narrative strategies found reflections in the chroniclers' selection and arrangement of topics. As noted throughout this study, the chronicles prioritized certain themes and events which contain information or teachings that contribute to the configuration of a distinct narrative approach to Observant reform. Glassberger favored saint lives and miracles attributed to Francis or other holy men; inspiring acts of devotion, asceticism, and missionary zeal; accounts of elections and official appointments; descriptions of councils; conflicts between Franciscan factions; martyrdoms of friars in Muslim lands; interactions with popes, bishops, cardinals and lay rulers; foundation histories of new provinces and friaries. For his part, Aquilano pays attention to conflict

---

364 Glassberger, *Chronicle*, 13.

narratives,[365] episodes of institutional history,[366] miracle narratives,[367] political and military histories,[368] to which he adds personal anecdotes.[369] In the following, I will look at the dominant narratives that appeared in the Observant chronicle writing and informed their discourse of reform: the narratives of events, the reports of conflicts, and biographies.

III.7.2. Narrative of events: from leadership-centered episodes to miracles

First, the chronicles deploy a wide range of episodes centered on representations of leadership external to the order, either ecclesiastical or political. This pattern is visible already at the beginning of Glassberger's chronicle which combines the portrayal of Saint Francis with aspects of the order's growth through both political maneuvering and miraculous interventions. In the year 1223, Saint Francis of Assisi sought to solidify the rule of his Order, after receiving divine guidance. He ascended a mountain with two companions and drafted the rule, which he later had to rewrite because it was lost. Despite initial concerns about its strictness, the rule was confirmed by Pope Honorius III in December of the same year. On this occasion, Glassberger emphasized that the drafting of the rule under divine revelation occurred simultaneously with leadership changes within the Order.[370]

Other extensive narratives involving leadership external to the Observance abounded. Glassberger details the events in the life of local kings like Bela of Hungary:

> Anno Domini 1270 Bela, rex Hungariae, germanus sanctae Elisabethae, quinto nonas Maii, hoc est in festo Inventionis sanctae Crucis, feliciter obiit, et paululum post mortem eius obiit etiam Maria regina, uxor

---

[365] Like Glassberger, Aquilano frequently describes conflicts between the Observants and Conventuals, or internal struggles within the Observant movement. This is evident in chapters 14 and 15 (*Chronicle* 47-53), which detail the "terrible war" against the Observant family in the Roman Curia.

[366] Aquilano focuses on important events in the Observant movement, such as general chapters and papal interventions. For instance, chapter 25 (*Chronicle*, 82-85) describes the events occurring in the general chapter in Milan in detail.

[367] While not as prominent as in Glassberger's case, Aquilano does include some accounts of miraculous events, such as the record of St. Bernardino's miracles (*Chronicle*, 37).

[368] Aquilano sometimes includes broader historical events that impacted the Franciscan order, such as the account of the battle against the Turks in chapter 24 (*Chronicle*, 78-81).

[369] Aquilano often includes firsthand accounts of events he witnessed or participated in. For example, he describes his own experience during a tense situation in Rome (*Chronicle*, 48-49).

[370] Glassberger, *Chronicle*, 31.

eius, Graeca, et Strigoniae in eccles ia Fratrum Minorum sunt sepulti. Horum corpora fecit Philippus, Archiepiscopus Strieoniensis, exhumari et contra iura in sua cathedrali ecclesia tumulari. Super quo facto causa coram Summo Pontifice diu ventilata, Fratres Minores eadem corpora cum honore ex integro rehabere meruerunt et ea coram Virginis ara gloriosius recondiderunt [...] Reliquit filium Stephanum quartum, qui fuit pater Mariae, matris sancti Ludovici, Episcopi Tolosani Ordinis nostri, et Roberti, regis Siciliae, et aliorum.

In the year of the Lord 1270, Bela, King of Hungary, brother of Saint Elizabeth, died peacefully on the fifth of the nones of May, that is, on the feast of the Finding of the Holy Cross. Shortly after his death, Queen Maria, his wife, who was Greek, also died, and they were buried in the church of the Franciscan Friars in Esztergom. Philip, Archbishop of Esztergom, had their bodies exhumed and, against legal rights, reburied in his cathedral church. This matter was debated for a long time before the Supreme Pontiff, and the Franciscan Friars deserved to fully recover these bodies with honor, and they reburied them more gloriously before the Virgin's altar [...] He left a son, Stephen IV, who was the father of Maria, mother of Saint Louis, Bishop of Toulouse of our Order, and of Robert, King of Sicily, and others.[371]

Later, in the same section, he recounts the death of King Louis of France, an event that impacted the development of the Observance:

Similiter obiit eodem anno christianissimus rex Francorum, Ludovicus, in peregrinatione ultra mare, et filius eius, nomine Iohannes. Navigaverat cum ipso rege ultra mare cruce signatus dominus Rigaldus, Archiepiscopus Rothomagensis et doctor Parisiensis Ordinis Minorum, in subsidium Terrae Sanctae, et multi Religiosi de Ordine Minorum et Praedicatorum, inter quos fuerunt frater Iohannes de Prisco et frater Walterus de Hoyo. Sed post mortem regis aliqui redierunt.

Similarly, in the same year [1270], the most Christian King Louis of France died during his pilgrimage overseas, along with his son named John. Lord Rigaud, Archbishop of Rouen and Paris doctor of the Order of Friars Minor, had sailed overseas with the king himself as a crusader in support

---

371 Glassberger, *Chronicle*, 82.

of the Holy Land, along with many Religious from the Orders of Friars Minor and Preachers, among whom were brother John of Prisco and brother Walter of Hoyo. But after the king's death, some returned.[372]

Connected to the events in the order's life, Glassberger alludes to other political events, like the coronation of Emperor Frederic II in 1220. The chronicle introduces this account in his broader narrative of a mission of three Franciscans and Saint Francis' return from overseas:

> Anno Domini 1220 Fridericus imperator „ huius nominis secundus, Romae coronatur in imperatorem in basilica sancti Petri de mandato domini Honorii Papae per ministerium domini Hugolini, tunc Episcopi Hostiensiset nostri Ordinis protectoris, ubi idem imperator de bonis et praediis imperii intra Italiam sitis multa contulit ecclesiae beati Petri , et votis accumulans, de manu eiusdem Episcopi Hostiensis rursus crucem accepit ad perficiendum iter Ierosolymitanum. Hoc autem anno, XVII. kalendas Februarii, pontificatus domini Honorii III. anno quarto, septem annis ante mortem sancti Francisci, quinque supradicti 3 fratres Marochium missi martyrium suum compleverunt. Reversus sanctus Franciscus de ultra mare, indixit capitulum generale.

> In the year of our Lord 1220, Emperor Frederick II, the second of that name, was crowned as emperor in the Basilica of Saint Peter in Rome by order of Pope Honorius, through the ministry of Bishop Hugolinus, who was then the Bishop of Ostia and our Order's protector. In the same year, the emperor generously bestowed many goods and properties within Italy to the Church of Saint Peter, accumulating blessings. He also received the cross from the same Bishop of Ostia to undertake the journey to Jerusalem. In this year, on the seventeenth day before February, during the fourth year of the pontificate of Pope Honorius III, seven years before the death of Saint Francis, the aforementioned three brothers completed their martyrdom in Morocco. Upon returning from overseas, Saint Francis convened a general chapter.[373]

Other times, he introduces political events that do not relate directly to Observant history, such as the rule and death of Albert, King of Hungary and Bohemia:

---

372 Glassberger, *Chronicle*, 82.
373 Glassberger, *Chronicle*, 18.

Eodem anno circa festum Simonis et Iudae obiit in Hungaria dominus Albertus, Romanorum, Hungariae et Bohemiae rex, cum solum duobus annis regnasset, et reliquit uxorem suam impraegnatam; ut nonnulli ferunt intoxicatus, alii autem dicunt profluvio veniris.

In the same year around the feast of Saints Simon and Jude [October 28], Lord Albert, King of the Romans, Hungary, and Bohemia, died in Hungary after reigning only two years, and left his wife pregnant; according to some he was poisoned, while others say it was due to dysentery.[374]

We also read about kings and princes who entered the monastic life, increasing the prestige of the monastic orders:

Eodem anno obtulerunt dominus Philippus, rex Franciae, et domina Iohanna, coniux eius, filiam suam, nomine Franciscam, beato Francisco et beatae Clarae virgini et eam in monasterio Longo Campo prope Parisius sub habitu et regula Minorissarum usque ad vitae terminum divino cultui dedicarunt.

In the same year, Lord Philip, King of France, and Lady Iohanna, his wife, offered their daughter, named Frances, to blessed Francis and blessed virgin Clare, and dedicated her to divine worship in the monastery of Longchamp near Paris under the habit and rule of the Poor Clares until the end of her life.[375]

Quite often, Glassberger also combines accounts of events in both political and ecclesiastical history:

Anno Domini 1440, in Cathedrae S. Petri festo electus est in regem Romanorum, Fridericus dominus, dux Austriae et Carinthiae et comes Tyroli, et diu distulit coronari propter schisma. Tandem, facta unione, coronatus est a Nicolao V. tempore Iubilaei. Eodem anno, subortis quibusdam dubiis inter Fratres, misit sanctus Bernardinus ipsis Fratribus praedictas declarationes fratris Nicolai de Auximo, inclusas in suis litteris talis tenoris.

---

374 Glassberger, *Chronicle*, 302.
375 Glassberger, *Chronicle*, 124.

In the year of our Lord 1440, on the feast of St. Peter's Chair, Lord Frederick, Duke of Austria and Carinthia and Count of Tyrol, was elected King of the Romans, and he long delayed his coronation because of the schism. Finally, after unity was achieved, he was crowned by Nicholas V during the Jubilee. In the same year, when certain doubts arose among the Brothers, Saint Bernardino sent to these Brothers the aforementioned declarations of Brother Nicholas of Osimo, enclosed in his letters of the following content.[376]

Most events function as a platform to connect the historical trajectory of the Observance with its spiritual and moral ideals, reinforcing the movement's identity and legitimacy within the Franciscan tradition. In the beginning, he points to the early Franciscans' experiences that occurred when moving to the German lands where they were accused of heresy. Glassberger highlights the challenges faced by the early Franciscan friars in establishing their identity and legitimacy. The lack of a written confirmation of their rule by Pope Innocent III, he asserts, made it difficult for the friars to be accepted in foreign lands.[377] A display of moralizing elements that emerge especially in the stories intended to present proofs of their institutional legitimation compensated this lack. The narrative of the Franciscan missions in *Theutonia*, for instance, not only showed the Franciscans' practical difficulties but also revealed their moral stance.[378]

If such accounts were common in a multitude of narratives, Observant chroniclers showed interest in combining narratives of events with miracles. Glassberger presents a compelling narrative of the encounter between Saint Francis and a servant possessed by a demon. The demon's inability to speak in the presence of Saint Francis served as a proof to the saint's spiritual power and authority, while the demon's subsequent speech provides a unique perspective on the role of the Franciscan Order in the history of salvation.[379] In other cases however, he reduces or eliminates any trace of miraculous elements from the source texts, presenting the saints as realistic and relatable figures rather than as unattainable models of holiness. The alternation between supernatural and humanized portrayals reflects a careful balancing of divine authority

---

376 Glassberger, *Chronicle*, 303.
377 Glassberger, *Chronicle*, 11.
378 Glassberger, *Chronicle*, 21.
379 Glassberger, *Chronicle*, 25-26.

with pastoral accessibility. This is the case with Glassberger's list of brief stories of miracles performed in Vienna in 1451:

> Transcripta miracula Viennae gesta sunt IX. Iunii, die mercurii: Fridericus Schreiber de Constantia in XV septimanis se movere sine duobus servis et ferulis non potuit; accepto signo crucis, dimisit omnia auxilia et ad ecclesiam ivit salvus et sanus.
>
> Anna, uxor Michaelis de Vienna, aetatis XL annorum, surda per XX annos, signata, mirifice auditum est consecuta.
>
> Catharina, uxor Michaelis Fieroth, Viennensis, paralytica per sex annos et sex menses, adeo ut per se ambulare non posset aliquo pacto, portata in sede et a Patre praeceptum suscipiens, ut surgeret in nomine Iesu Christi benedicti, statim surrexit ac per se libera incessit.
>
> Anna, uxor Conradi Ulnatoris de Vienna, XII annis caeca, signata, statim illuminata est, ut omnes colores mirifice discerneret.
>
> Catharina, uxor magistri Nicolai, chirurgici Viennensis, XL annorum, per VII hebdomadas immobilis et destituta viribus, portata in una cathedra, signata per Patrem, per se incessit libera, relicta cathedra, domum pedibus propriis ivit, ac si nunquam malum habuisset.

> The following miracles were recorded in Vienna on Wednesday, June 9: Frederick Schreiber from Constance could not move for 15 weeks without two servants and crutches; after receiving the sign of the cross, he abandoned all aids and went to church safe and sound.
>
> Anna, wife of Michael from Vienna, aged 40 years, deaf for 20 years, after being signed, miraculously regained her hearing.
>
> Catherine, wife of Michael Fieroth of Vienna, paralyzed for six years and six months, such that she could not walk by herself in any way, was carried in a chair and, receiving the Father's command to rise in the name of blessed Jesus Christ, immediately stood up and walked freely by herself.

Anna, wife of Conrad the Weaver from Vienna, blind for 12 years, upon being signed, was immediately given sight, such that she could miraculously distinguish all colors.

Catherine, wife of Master Nicholas, a Viennese surgeon, aged 40, immobile and without strength for 7 weeks, was carried in a chair, and after being signed by the Father, walked freely by herself, leaving the chair behind, went home on her own feet as if she had never been ill.[380]

These illustrations suggest that the chronicles' narratives of events were intended to convey spiritual authenticity both through adherence to the Franciscan Rule and by responding to popular devotional practices. By contrasting the exemplary virtues of Observant leaders with the perceived laxity of their counterparts and strategically using miracle stories, these narratives constructed a historical-spiritual basis that justifies the Observant cause. This deliberate juxtaposition serves not only to point to the righteousness of the Observants but also to admonish deviations from their strict practices. Through moralization and miracle accounts, the chronicles portrayed the Observants as bearers of spiritual integrity, ordained to lead and reform. They reinforced the Observant legitimacy and the moral-spiritual grounding in popular contexts within religious and political contexts.

III.7.3. Narrative of conflicts

Beside the accounts of events, another pervasive type of narrative emerging in the chronicles pertains to solving conflicts and tensions. Such stories generated much of the chronicles' dynamic drive in the representation of reform. Bernardino Aquilano's *Chronicle* begins with a narrative of a conflict between a group of "good brothers" who planned to gather to observe the rule which, according to them, had declined, and another group opposing this move. The author casts this situation in terms of a battle with "the devil" and an act of persecution, emphasizing the tension between the advocates of a stricter observance and those comfortable with looser practices of religious observance. The emphasis in this conflict on the persecuted brothers serves Aquilano to trace the history of Observance by representing the earliest adherents and proponents of the Observant reform movement. Their dispersal also hints at the challenges which reformers faced from the very beginning.

---

[380] Glassberger, *Chronicle*, 338 (and *passim*).

Like Glassberger's chronicle but with other means, Aquilano's narrative situates the Observant reform movement in a reaction against declining regular observance in the order.[381]

Aquilano's focus remains on conflicts involving early proponents of Observance who were forced to separate from other Franciscans because of conflicts and hostility. Among the first Franciscans dissatisfied with the observance of Saint Francis' rule, Aquilano identifies Angelo da Clareno (1247-1337) and suggests that he faced serious persecution for his strictness in the interpretation of Franciscan precepts.[382] The chronicler paints Angelo's personality in positive terms that emphasize his sanctity and divine favor, like the miraculous acquisition of Greek language which he used to translate the popular text of John Climacus' *Ladder* into Latin. Angelo's story demonstrates the role of the conflict narratives in the construction of a vision about the Observance. The translations, the dissemination of spiritual knowledge, and the education were additional themes that reinforced the Observant views in the conflicts between different Franciscan factions and specifically in the competition between Observants and Conventuals. To escape persecution, Angelo eventually left the Franciscan Order, adopting a hermit's habit and living under episcopal authority until the time of Pope Sixtus IV.[383]

As the beginning of the chronicle emphasizes the challenges and persecutions faced by those who sought to live according to the strict interpretation of the Franciscan rule, the themes of persecution and conflict surface in Observant writings. Both chronicles abound in narratives of conflicts with the Conventuals. Glassberger details the initial tensions with the Conventuals which later were reignited:

> Anno Domini 1445, defuncto magistro Gulielmo de Casali, Generali Ministro, anno sui generalatus XII, Eugenius Papa, volens iterum reformationem Ordinis aggredi, instituit Vicarium Ordinis fratrem Albertum de Sarthiano, magnae sanctitatis et scientiae virum regularisque observantiae zelantissimum, concessisque ei quibusdam facultatibus per Bullas Apostolicas, capitulum generale eodem anno Paduae celebrari iussit, intendens et sperans, quod idem frater Albertus in eodem capitulo in Generalem Ministrum elegeretur. Congregato autem capitulo generali totius Ordinis, tam Conventualium quam

---

381 Aquilano, *Chronicle*, 2-3.
382 Aquilano, *Chronicle*, 4.
383 Aquilano, *Chronicle*, 5.

de Observantia, cum in ipso capitulo dictae facultates legerentur, Conventuales clamabant: 'Libertas, libertas'. Et tumultum facientes, ipsum fratrem Albertum de Sarthiano, Vicarium totius Ordinis, arrepta ei capsula Bullarum, de loco capituli vi ad extra conclavium portaverunt.

In the year of the Lord 1445, after the death of Master William of Casale, Minister General, in the twelfth year of his generalate, Pope Eugenius, wishing to undertake another reform of the Order, appointed Brother Albert of Sarteano as Vicar of the Order, a man of great holiness and learning and most zealous for regular observance. Having granted him certain faculties through Apostolic Bulls, he ordered a general chapter to be held that same year in Padua, intending and hoping that the same Brother Albert would be elected Minister General in that chapter. However, when the general chapter of the whole Order, both Conventuals and Observants, was assembled, and when these said faculties were being read in the chapter, the Conventuals shouted: "Freedom, freedom!" And causing a tumult, they forcibly carried Brother Albert of Sarteano himself, Vicar of the whole Order, out of the chapter room beyond the enclosure, having seized from him the case containing the Bulls.[384]

Glassberger's chronicle, on the other hand, did not limit itself to internal conflicts but also detailed military conflicts with external forces, particularly the Ottomans. He describes the events surrounding the Battle of Belgrade in 1456, where Christian forces, led by John Hunyadi, defended the city against the Ottoman Turks led by Sultan Mehmed II. The chronicle recounts how in 1456, John Capistrano, while sailing down the Danube to aid in the defense of Belgrade, received a divine vision encouraging him to proceed fearlessly. Despite facing overwhelming odds against the Turkish forces, which boasted 120,000 men on land and sixty-four large ships on the Danube, the Christian defenders placed their faith in God and John's leadership. During the battle on July 22, John led the crusaders out of the castle, invoking Jesus' name. He remained unharmed as Turkish arrows and stones flew around him. The Christians, under the joint coordination of John Hunyadi and John Capistrano, won. Turkish captives reported hearing voices crying out *Jesus* in the air. Pope Callixtus III later recounted that 40,000 Turks were killed, with an equal number fleeing and turning on each other. The wounded Sultan hastily retreated to Constantinople. This extraordinary triumph was preceded by the appearance of a large

---

[384] Glassberger, *Chronicle*, 308.

star with a bright cross above it near the earth, interpreted as a sign of divine favor. The day after the battle, the Christians collected the weapons and defenses left behind by the fleeing Turks, including five ships filled with arms, gold, and silver. The spoils, Glassberger notes, were kept in the castle for the common good and necessity of present and future Christians. The bodies of the dead *infidels* were removed and thrown into the Danube River for four continuous days. The bodies of the Christians who died in the battle were collected with devotion and veneration, and buried in the church of Saint Michael with hymns and praises. Glassberger's reproduction of Capistrano's letter detailing the victory emphasized the role of divine intervention in overcoming such formidable odds. The chronicle further emphasizes the role of the divine in the battle when noting that the star with the cross remained above the Christian camp for the entire day and night, moving with them and providing unwavering light until they returned to their tents.[385]

The same combination of historical events deriving from military conflicts and divine intervention is present in Glassberger's recounting of John Hunyadi's actions during the conflict with the Ottomans. The same Glassberger describes a vision experienced by Hunyadi the night following the battle which troubled him because of the deaths of many Christians, who were not killed by conventional weapons, but trampled by horses and camels. In this vision, he saw a priest celebrating Mass, while during the Offertory, each person was signed with the cross by the priest and took a seat on the altar. At the Sanctus, a mighty king and queen arrived with a great retinue of ministers, who received those seated on the altar and joined them. After the Mass, the king and the queen led the others away, saying, "Come, blessed of my Father." John Capistrano interpreted the vision, explaining that the priest represents the Pope, who has the power to bind and loose, and who sent legates and cardinals to preach the remission of sins to those who fought or contributed to the battle. Those who accepted this preaching or sent others at their own expense were those seen going to the Offertory, and were fortified with the sign of the cross by Pope Callixtus III through his legates.[386]

These details and accompanying stories of conflicts with which Glassberger describes the battle signal a change in the construction of Observant chronicle narratives. If in most chronicles, including Aquilano's, the conflicts presented were often internal, Glassberger zooms out to

---

385   Glassberger, *Chronicle*, 364-368.
386   Glassberger, *Chronicle*, 365.

wide-reaching situations, offering the Observance historical relevance. Such conflicts of significant magnitude were meant not only to present the Observant contribution to the divinely sanctioned victories for the Christian forces that halted the Ottoman advance into Europe for several decades but also to highlight the role played by influential leaders in securing such outcomes. The chronicler singles out John Capistrano as a skilled diplomat and defender of the cause of Christian liberty and unity.[387] This was emblematic of how, in the chronicles, the agency and leadership of prominent individuals were instrumental in resolving conflicts, demonstrating that the prowess of key figures could sway the tides of war and ensure the preservation of the order.

III.7.4. Biographies

The narratives of conflicts shaped by personalities like Capistrano suggest the chronicles conceived Observant legitimization as a process that hinged on balancing individual charisma and communal adherence to the Franciscan Rule. Chronicles balanced the demands of a reform that attended to the influence of several individuals with the stability of tradition reflected in their identity. In this respect, the biographical portrayals serve as another key instrument in constructing this dynamic identity, revealing the inherent tension between individuality and collectivity.

The biographical approach is evident in the chronicles' treatment of key figures like Saint Francis, Bernardino of Siena, and John Capistrano. If Saint Francis serves as the foundational figure for the Franciscan tradition, in the Observant chronicles his portrayal takes on particular traits. Glassberger emphasizes Francis' strict adherence to poverty and humility, presenting him as the ultimate model for Observant emulation. Other figures like Bernardino of Siena emerge as pivotal in the consolidation of the Observant movement. Aquilano and Glassberger highlight Bernardino's role as charismatic preacher, skilled administrator, and defender of Observant autonomy. The chronicles present moments in Bernardino's life as central to the Observance, especially his appointment as Vicar in Tuscany, and later as Vicar General over the Observant Friars in Italy. Under Bernardino's leadership, Glassberger shows, the Observants experienced substantial growth in both the number of friars and houses, not only in Italy but also in other regions.[388]

---

387 Glassberger, *Chronicle*, 366.
388 Glassberger, *Chronicle,* 278.

However, these portrays were not devoid of controversies and conflicts. Glassberger acknowledges the issues surrounding Bernardino's reforms, including the opposition of Conventual Franciscans and disagreements among the Observants themselves. This nuanced portrayal reveals the challenges inherent in approaching the sensitive issues of the complex landscape of Franciscan politics and the delicate balance required to maintain unity within a rapidly growing movement. Bernardino's eventual canonization, as recounted by Glassberger, serves as a validation of the Observant reform and solidifies his status as a model of Observant virtues.

In the footsteps of Bernardino's presentation, John Capistrano emerges as another key figure in the Observant expansion. Glassberger emphasizes Capistrano's tireless preaching, his success in converting Hussites, and influence on powerful figures like Emperor Frederick III. In dealing with Capistrano, Glassberger proceeds not from his early career but from the year 1451, when the preacher, together with twelve companions, embarked on a journey to *Alamannia*, an endeavor which he frames as set up by the example of Christ. Glassberger provides a detailed list of his companions, that includes the Gabriel of Verona, Jerome of Milan, and Nicholas of Fara, who later became Vicars of the Provinces. Among the lay companions were Bernard of Naples, Paul of Ferrara, and Michael of Prussia. Glassberger emphasizes the diverse backgrounds of these companions and, above all, the universal appeal of John of Capistrano's mission.[389] While Glassberger does not provide a full-fledged biography of Capistrano, he includes key details about his life and work, particularly his missionary journeys and his role in the Battle of Belgrade.

A lengthy letter praising Capistrano's virtues and recounting his death further underscores his career within the Observant narrative. Even if introduced only at the end of the account of Capistrano's life, the letter is telling for the attempt to promote Capistrano's figure as a worthy successor to Saint Francis:

> Igitur servus Christi, beatus Iohannes de Capistrano, post peractum bellum contra Turcum propter immensos labores, quos sustinuit, cum iam esset LXXI annorum, aegrotare coepit dixitque sociis: 'Adhuc non sum certus, utrum hac aegritudine moriturus sim, sed tali die certificabor'; qua adveniente, dixit sociis suis, se esse moriturum. Et quia Fratres Hungari, qui tunc sub Generali Vicario cismontano erant, se difficiles reddebant in suscipiendo conventu in Illoca cum tamen haberent super

---

[389] Glassberger, *Chronicle*, 332-353.

hoc litteras Apostolicas, iussit se Pater ad eundem conventum deferri, dicens: 'Postquam in illo moriar, Fratres de Observantia amplius conventum non dimittent.' Delatus ergo ad praedictum locum, per plures dies valida fluxus aegritudine laboravit, ita ut nihil relinere posset. Quam infirmitatem patientissime, semper Deo gratias agens, sustinuit, nec unquam ab oratione vacans, divinum officium, usquequo potuit os aperire, persolvit. Postremo stipendia vitae flagitans, confiteri, novissime communicari, perungi et animam Deo committi voluit, non in stratu, non in mollibus, non in deliciis, sed in pavimento iacens; nihilominus, quasi ceteri, pro se ipso deprecans: 'Sancta Maria, ora pro me, sancte Abraham, ora pro me', et cetera referens cum reverentia, cunctis astantibus attentior, sic quod minus bene proferentem ac barbarizantem hebdomadarium saepius corriperet emendaretque. Superfuit post hoc per dies VII, uno dumtaxat ovi vitello ac tribus uvarum granis confotus. Sabbato itaque, quo etiam obiit beatus Franciscus, dum primum ad Vesperas daretur signum, perfectae mentis compos ac sensu vivax, socium nutu advocans auxilii ferendi gratia, sedere voluit, et inclinando ad pectus eius titubans, caput suaviter, ore sensim aperio, inter ulnas ei exanime corpus reliquit. Obiit autem vir Dei anno Domini MCCCCLVI, die XXIII. Octobris, in oppido Illoca, regni Hungariae, sepultus.

Therefore Christ's servant, blessed John Capistrano, after completing the war against the Turk, began to fall ill due to the immense labors he had endured, being already 71 years old. He said to his companions: "I am not yet certain whether I will die from this illness, but on such a day I will know for certain." When that day came, he told his companions that he would die. And because the Hungarian Friars, who were then under the Cismontane Vicar General, were being difficult about accepting the convent in Ilok despite having Apostolic letters concerning this, the Father ordered himself to be carried to that same convent, saying: "After I die there, the Observant Friars will no longer give up the convent." Having been carried to the aforementioned place, he suffered for several days from a severe illness with flux, such that he could retain nothing. He endured this infirmity most patiently, always giving thanks to God, never ceasing from prayer, and reciting the divine office as long as he could open his mouth. Finally, requesting the provisions for life's end, he wished to confess, receive final communion, be anointed, and commend his soul to God, lying not on a bed, not on soft things, not in comfort, but on the floor. Nevertheless, like others, praying for himself: "Holy Mary, pray for me, Saint Abraham, pray for me," and continuing with reverence, more attentive than all those present, so much so that he would often correct and amend the weekly officiant who was pronouncing poorly and speaking barbarously. He lived for seven days after this, sustained only by one egg yolk and three grape seeds. And so on Saturday, when blessed Francis also died, while the first signal for Vespers was being given, being in full possession of his mind and alert in his senses, beckoning his companion to help him, he wanted to sit up, and leaning his wavering head against his companion's chest, gently, with his mouth slightly open, he left his lifeless body in his arms. The man of God died in the year of the Lord 1456, on October 23, in the town of Ilok, in the kingdom of Hungary, where he was buried.[390]

Still, if both Aquilano and Glassberger employ biographical elements, their approaches differ significantly, reflecting their respective visions of the Observant project. Of all the Observant chroniclers, Aquilano appears to make extensive use of the biographical form. He groups together biographical snippets from the lives of the important Observants from the turn of the fourteenth century: Giovanni da Stroncone, Bartholomaeus de Jano, Franciscus de Trevio, Albertus de Sarthiano, John Capistrano, James of Marches, and Albert of Calabria. Aquilano populates his chronicle with a diverse cast of characters, ranging from prominent figures to lesser-known friars like Seraphinus de Gaeta, described in few words as "vir valens et bonus" or characters speaking mostly through sermons intended to stress the moralizing character of the text.[391] Although brief, such character sketches contribute to the moralizing tone of Aquilano's chronicle and highlight individual piety within the Observant movement.

Glassberger, on the other hand, adopts a restrained approach to individual characterization. His focus lies on the integration of individual agency into an official narrative of the Order's development. Acknowledging the contributions of individual figures, he tends to subsume them under a framework of institutional progress, emphasizing the roles of popes, cardinals, and other officials in shaping the Observant trajectory. This emphasis on institutional actors reflects Glassberger's concern with establishing the Observance's legitimacy within the existing power structures of the Church.

Glassberger's seemingly impersonal approach does not prevent the strategic deployment of individual exemplars. Occasionally, he draws

---

390   Glassberger, *Chronicle*, 371-372.
391   Aquilano, *Chronicle*, 43.

parallels between key figures in the Observant movement and biblical or saintly characters like David, Moses, John the Baptist, or the prophets, using typology to reinforce their authority and underscore the divinely ordained nature of the Observant reform. The figure of King David, for example, is invoked to legitimize the Observants' political aspirations, drawing a connection between David's foundational work in establishing the Israelite kingdom and the Observants' efforts to consolidate their own position within the Franciscan Order.[392] This typological approach allows Glassberger to assert the Observants' claim to spiritual and institutional authority without overly emphasizing individual personalities.

Whether individualized like in Aquilano's chronicle or presented through a typological-institutional lens like in Glassberger's, the biographical accounts point to a dialectical construction of Observant identity. Arguably, the portrayal of individual figures stood at the intersection of the narrative types discussed above. We see them closely correlated with narratives reflecting Franciscan identity and of historical events where rulers or popes take decisions. We also see individuals involved in tense polemics which erupt into local or regional conflicts. But chronicle biographies also tap into the benefits of other elements in the chronicles. For instance, Glassberger's inclusion of letters also reinforced a dialectical understanding of identity. The epistles embedded in the chronicles, provide glimpses into the lived experiences of individual Observants and their interactions with other institutional actors. As complementary to the biographies, epistolary communication underlines the relationships between individuals and other groups as well as the internal debates about the direction of reform.

These illustrations serve as further evidence for embedding biographies, a widely used genre in the promotion of the Observance, in the framework of the chronicles' institutional history. As hagiographical snippets or accounts of exemplary figures, such as church and political leaders, biographies were integrated into the chronicles' account of institutional history. Through biographical details chroniclers framed individuals as heroes or adversaries in the context of the Observant movement's struggles. This distinct narrative strategy rooted in other source texts like saints' lives helped to define the Observant identity in opposition to those who opposed or undermined their reforms. Biographies also reinforced the idea of Observant origins. For example, in Aquilano's chronicle, the life of Paulutius of Foligno is tied to the early efforts to

---

392 Glassberger, *Chronicle*, 160, 294, 424.

establish stricter observance of the Franciscan rule, and his story is used to explain the origins and growth of the Observant movement.[393] The text moves between individual lives and the collective history of the order, showing how personal actions influenced institutional developments.[394] But a key ingredient in fusing biography and institutional history appears to be the treatment of foundational figures. Chronicles use biographical passages to mark moments in the order's history, such as the establishment of new communities, the spread of the Observant reform, and the defense of the order against internal and external challenges. If Saint Francis plays the role of a protagonist only in Glassberger's narrative, the interest in John Capistrano and Bernardino of Siena is shared by both chroniclers. For instance, Capistrano's efforts to defend the Observants against their detractors are recounted in detail, linking his personal struggles to the institutional conflicts of the time. Such uses of biographical materials can be seen also at other levels of the narrative, as in the use of biographies to connect the past with the present, showing how the actions of earlier Observants laid the groundwork for the current state of the order. This created a sense of continuity, reinforcing the identity of the Observant movement as a legitimate inheritor of the original Franciscan ideal. Biographies instilled further dynamism to the narrative especially in the narration of conflicts as with Aquilano's account of Robert of Lecce whose eventual departure from the Observants to join the Conventuals is presented as a cautionary tale, highlighting the dangers of ambition and disunity.[395]

III.7.5. Observant history: a dynamic enterprise and a story of continuity

The combinations of the narrative types identified above allow us to draw further conclusions about the changing nature and role of chronicles in the formation of the discourse of reform in correlation to the formation of Observant identity. Even if they employed distinct strategies, chronicles drew on the same body of information and pursued similar goals. This comprehensiveness turned Observant identity into a discursive nexus, a textual framework where the rigor of official documents, the moralizing tone of the sermons, and anecdotal recounting intersected. With their marked differences, the two chronicles examined here show that, in the

---

[393] Aquilano, *Chronicle*, 6-7.
[394] Aquilano, *Chronicle*, 8-10.
[395] Aquilano, *Chronicle*, 38-42.

attempt to solidify their position within the late medieval Church, the Observants employed historical narratives not to record their history, but to actively shape their identity as a group involved in public affairs and concomitantly promote a reformist agenda within and beyond the order.

Significantly, the chronicles' version of Observant identity emphasized continuity: of action between past and present as well as of the communication medium. In a single framework, they bridged existing raw information drawn from factual accounts with the moralization embedded in the ethical interpretations. The choice of narrative form reflects an understanding of the prevailing religious discourse as holding historical background, legal grounding, and divinely sanctioned acts of reform. By presenting themselves as inheritors of the Franciscan legacy, they sought to gain legitimacy and authority within an increasingly competitive religious landscape where reforming movements were vying for influence. To this extent, the chronicles became carefully constructed expressions of a vision of Franciscan life, emphasizing their connection to the past while differentiating themselves from other branches of the order. This involved establishing a distinct legal and institutional grounding for their reforms, demonstrated through papal endorsements, decrees from Church councils, and the help of influential personalities. The chronicles show that the Observants understood that achieving recognition and acceptance required the formulation of a new perspective on the connections between spiritual authority and secular power.

The chronicles' conception of history was not a neutral recounting of facts, but a purposeful work designed to explain and display their growth. Miraculous interventions served as evidence of divine favor, validating claims to spiritual authenticity. The chroniclers placed their narratives within a distinct moral sphere, highlighting the main virtues of Observant leaders, obedience, austerity, and charity, and implicitly criticizing the perceived laxity of their rivals. The biographies and other narratives of episodes allowed them to illustrate these virtues by presenting exemplary figures, offering concrete models for emulation and reinforcing the narrative of their movement's divinely ordained growth. This approach not only underscored the importance of individual piety and leadership but also connected these individuals to a historical trajectory, portraying the Observant movement as a force of renewal within the Franciscan order and the Church at large.

The Observant chronicles, therefore, should be understood as tools of persuasion, akin to the medieval *specula* meant to educate inasmuch as to advance the movement's goals within the religious and political landscape of the later Middle Ages. By offering a pedagogical model aligned to other Observant pedagogical efforts, they represented a conscious effort to discursively recreate the narrative of Franciscan history, positioning the Observants as the true heirs of Saint Francis and the rightful leaders of a reformed Franciscan order.[396] Also, by weaving together historical accounts, theological arguments, and stories from the inside of the order, the chroniclers constructed a case for their vision of Franciscan life, contributing to their success in establishing themselves as a distinct group within the late medieval Church.

Much of this success stemmed from the ability to modulate their discourse in order to resonate with diverse audiences and specific contexts. Aquilano, writing for an internal monastic audience, adopted a personal and anecdotal style, emphasizing the struggles and triumphs of individual Observants. His focus on biographical portrayals and narratives of conflict created a sense of shared identity based on relatable figures who, despite adversities, remained steadfast in their commitments. On the other hand, Glassberger, writing at a time of increasing Observant influence, adopted a more comprehensive approach tracing institutional history. With an emphasis on historical events, his chronicle aimed to establish the Observants' legitimacy within the Church and society. By emphasizing papal endorsements, documenting institutional growth, and situating the Observant movement within the context of Franciscan history, he sought to secure the order's position within established power structures. Furthermore, his use of typological profiles, linking Observant figures to biblical and historical exemplars, elevated their status and reinforced their claim to spiritual authority.

The differences between Aquilano and Glassberger's chronicles reveal an adaptation to the changing priorities of the Observant movement. Aquilano's chronicle, written during a period of internal consolidation, focused on strengthening the order's internal cohesion and reinforcing its core values. Glassberger's later chronicle, reflecting the Observants' growing prominence, shifted towards external legitimation and the consolidation of their position within the religious and political landscape of late medieval Europe. This shift in focus demonstrates the Observants' evolving strategies for self-preservation and advancement, adapting their historical approach to meet the challenges of their time.

---

396   See also Roest (1997).

Conclusion
Narrative constructions of Observant identity: between action and ideals

In answering to both internal and external challenges, chronicles picture the Observant reform as a phenomenon with trans-regional and institutional ramifications. Originating in the Italian peninsula, the Franciscan Observance spread across Europe, taking root in diverse regional and political contexts. Observant communities established close ties and networks that strengthened the exchange of ideas, people, and best practices. This allowed the Observants to coordinate their reform efforts on a trans-regional scale, drawing on shared strategies that transcended local boundaries. The Observant message resonated with devout populations in Iberia, France, the Low Countries, Germany, and beyond, as friars used preaching, textual production, and lay outreach to cultivate their vision of religious renewal. Many chronicles documented this rapid diffusion, showing the Observants' ability to adapt their discourse and practices to local environments while maintaining a cohesive identity.

The main sources of this study, Aquilano's and Glassberger's chronicles, offer detail-rich accounts of Observant life. They make up both historical records and arguments for a particular understanding of Franciscan life and identity rooted in the literal preservation of Francis' ideals. The diversity of people, places, and events covered offers a panoramic view of a slice of Franciscan history. The chronicles also reveal much about their authors' own literary personality and style, the intellectual currents of their time, and a view of religious and ethnic otherness that is more balanced than in moralizing sermons and more comprehensive than in letters or documents.

The argument of this study revolves around the idea that the Observants employed historical narratives as discursive tools to construct and promote a distinct identity. This was a dynamic identity correlated to the general agenda for religious reform centered on virtues and church unity. Through these identity narratives, the Observants sought to shape public perception and legitimize their movement as part of the context of late medieval religious and intellectual life and present it as mediating conflicts and tensions. As a medium of communication designed for internal monastic audiences, chronicles relied on linear narrative continuity that set them apart from dialectic or dialogic genres like sermons or letters. This linearity allowed chroniclers to expand the scope of their public presence and present a coherent representation of the growth and legitimacy of the Observance. By addressing the complexities of their historical moment, they merged distinct sources (stories, sermons, letters, decrees) in a mixed form that offered a panoramic representation of the order.

Within the process of configuring Observant identity, the narratives served multiple purposes: they articulated the Observants' ideals of poverty, humility, and adherence to the original Franciscan Rule, becoming a tool of educating Observant communities; they provided exemplary models of virtuous behavior and sanctity; they established a sense of continuity with the Order's origins while distancing the Observants from perceived laxities of other religious factions like the Conventuals; and they adapted their language and rhetoric to reach diverse audiences, from fellow monastics to lay believers. All in all, Bernardino Aquilano and Nicholas Glassberger's narratives reflect the convergence of religious, political, and intellectual ideas or practices of the late medieval period.

By connecting the various sources of Observant history and enriching the reform discourse models of individuals and key events, chronicles signaled existing textual communities where ideas were confronted, nuanced, and disseminated. They reveal the Observants' engagement with political and social structures, despite their lack of a crystallized political or economic doctrine. Both Aquilano and Glassberger depict the Observants as mediators between political factions, emphasizing their role in promoting unity and stability, in support of monarchs and the papacy. This political dimension underscores the chroniclers' predilection for legitimizing events and displaying internal cohesion, while downplaying interactions with other intellectual groups like the Humanism.

The present exploration therefore showed that Observant chroniclers should be evaluated against the late medieval intellectual and political landscape, balancing the need for official texts, preaching, and saintly models to address diverse audiences with the imperative to uphold their virtue system and reform agenda. Even if embedding heavy historical documentation, they also encompassed an argument for the Observants' autonomy from ongoing intellectual developments or institutional structures. The selective approach to historical material and information (sometimes expanding and sometimes abbreviating it) reflects the chroniclers' focus on internal and legitimizing events, as well as their commitment to reinforcing the Observants' distinctive social identity and separation from their religious peers. Their view of the past was also distinguished from other similar monastic chronicles, a widespread genre in the later Middle Ages. What distinguished the Franciscan Observants was that they perceived the past not as a succession of exemplary figures or moral precepts, as was common in Dominican chronicles for instance, but in relation to the surrounding social, political, and economic conditions.[397] This approach allowed Observant chroniclers to present their reform as a practical solution to contemporary problems, rather than as a set of abstract ideals.

The chronicles not only were influenced by the discourse of Observant reform, as developed in other texts, but also sought to reinterpret it, adapting their themes to address the challenges of a changing political and intellectual landscape. They made heavy use of miracles in their accounts of key episodes of the order's development such as the councils, or in their stories about resolutions of conflicts. Such thematic versatility helped the Observants to define their identity by addressing other issues like the obstacles encountered and the engagement with the "other".

The chronicles thus suggest that the discourse of Observance reform represented a phenomenon combining layers of spiritual experience, historical continuity, and practical adaptation. The monastic records of Glassberger and Aquillano fulfilled the function of the community's *lieu de mémoire*, affirming identities with both local and general dimensions. The differences of approach between the chronicles indicate that far from a monolithic group, the Observance emerged as a community comprising multiple branches, reflecting a laborious process of formation over several centuries, from the late fourteenth to the early sixteenth century. This situation aligned with the reality of its geographic extent, since the

---

397 Hujbers (2020), 214-215.

Observant movement assumed distinct features in each of the regions of its distribution, whether in Italy or beyond its borders. The regional diversity, coupled with the shared commitment to education and reform across several critical decades, revealed the richness and complexity of the chronicles as both historical records and tools for religious and political transformation.

Bibliography

Primary Sources:

Bernardino Aquilano. *Chronica fratrum minorum observantiae*. Ed. L. Lemmens, Rome: Salustiani, 1902.

Bernardino Aquilano. *Chronica fratrum minorum observantiae*. Ed. L. Pellegrini, Milan: Biblioteca Francescana, 2021.

Bernardinus Senensis. *Pro scholaribus septem disciplinae*. In *Bernardini Senensis Opera omnia*, vol. IX. Florence: Quaracchi, 1963. 406–408.

Cristopher Varese, *Vita di fra Giovanni da Capestrano*. Ed. and trans. Michele Antonio di Loreto, L'Aquila, 1988.

Eberhard Ablauff de Rheno. *De novella plantatione provincie Austrie, Bohemie et Polonie quoad fratres Minores de Observantia*. Edited by Antonín Kalous and Jana Svobodová. Rome: Viella, 2024.

Giaccomo Oddi. *La Franceschina: Testo volgare Umbro del sec. XV*. 2 vols. Ed. N. Cavna, S. Maria degli Angeli-Assisi: Tipogralia Porziuncola, 1929.

John Capistrano. *Correspondence. Letters Related to the History of Poland and Silesia (1451-1456)*. Ed. Paweł Kras, Halina Manikowska, Marcin Starzyński, Anna Zajchowska-Bołtromiuk, in cooperation with Maria Koczerska, Marek D. Kowalski, Mieczysław Mejor, Letizia Pellegrini, Stephen Rowell, Filippo Sedda, translated into English by Stephen Rowell, Warsaw: Wydawnictwo KUL, 2018.

John of Komorowo, *Breve memoriale ordinis Fratrum Minorum*. Ed. by K. Liske and A. Loriciewicz, Monumenta Poloniae Historica 5, 1888.

Michael of Carinthia. *Chronica Fratrum minorum de Observancia provincie Bohemie*. Knihovna národního muzea [KNM] (Prague, Library of the national Museum), ms. VIII F 75, p. 1–455. (Modern edition in preparation by Antonín Kalous and Kateřina Ptáčková).

Nicholas of Fara, *Vita clarissimi viri fratris Joannis de Capistrano (BHL 4360), AASS* Octobris 10 (1861), 439–83.

Nicolaus Glassberger. *Chronica fratris Nicolai Glassberger ordinis minorum observantium.* Florence: Quaracchi, 1887.

Tucher, Sixtus. *Vierzig Sendbriefe aus dem Latein in das Teutsch gezogen.* Nuremberg, 1515.

Secondary Literature:

Bainton, Henry. 2018. Epistolary Documents in High-Medieval History-Writing. *Interfaces: A Journal of Medieval European Literatures* 4: 9–38.

Banker, James. 1988. *Death in the Community: Memorialization and Confraternities in an Italian Commune in the Late Middle Ages.* Athens GA: University of Georgia Press.

Barker, Paula. 1990. *'A Mirror of Piety and Learning': Caritas Pirckheimer Against the Reformation.* Ph.D. dissertation, University of Chicago.

Barker, Paula. 1995. "Caritas Pirckheimer: A Female Humanist Confronts the Reformation." *The Sixteenth Century Journal* 26 (2): 259–72.

Baron, Hans. 1938. "Franciscan Poverty and Civic Wealth as Factors in the Rise of Humanistic Thought." *Speculum* 13: 1–37.

Bast, Robert. 1997. *Honor Your Fathers: Catechisms and the Emergence of a Patriarchal Ideology in Germany, 1400-1600.* Leiden: Brill.

Bateson, Mary. 1894. "The Supposed Latin Penitential of Egbert and the Missing Work of Halitgar of Cambrai." *The English Historical Review* 9, no. 34: 320–26.

Baumgartner, Frederic. 2003. *Behind Locked Doors: A History of the Papal Elections.* London: Palgrave Macmillan.

Bejczy, István. 2011. *The Cardinal Virtues in the Middle Ages.* Leiden, The Netherlands: Brill.

Bisaha, Nancy. 2004. *Creating East and West Renaissance Humanists and the Ottoman Turks.* Philadelphia: University of Pennsylvania Press.

Bisaha, Nancy. 2023. *From Christians to Europeans: Pope Pius II and the Concept of the Modern Western Identity.* London: Routledge.

Bistoni, Maria Grazia. 1973. "La biblioteca del convento francescano di Monteripido in Perugia." *Archivum Franciscanum Historicum* 66: 378–404.

Bornstein, Daniel E. 1993. "Giovanni Dominici, the Bianchi, and Venice: Symbolic Action and Interpretive Grids." *The Journal of Medieval and Renaissance Studies* 23, no. 2: 143–171.

Bowman, Robert. 2014. *The Avignon Papacy, 1305-1378*. Oxford University Press.

Bratu, Cristian. 2019. *Je, auteur de ce livre. L'affirmation de soi chez les historiens, de l'Antiquité à la fin du Moyen Age*. Leiden: Brill.

Brundage, James. 2008. *The Medieval Origins of the Legal Profession: Canonists, Civilians, and Courts*. Chicago: University of Chicago Press.

Bruni, Francesco. 2003. *La città divisa: Le parti e il bene comune da Dante a Guicciardini*. Bologna: Il Mulino.

Bruzelius, Caroline. 2004. *The Stones of Naples: Church Building in Angevin Italy, 1266-1343*. New Haven: Yale University Press.

Camargo, Martin. 1988. "Toward a Comprehensive Art of Written Discourse: Geoffrey of Vinsauf and the Ars Dictaminis." *Rhetorica: A Journal of the History of Rhetoric* 6: 167–94.

Cannon, James, and Vauchez, André, eds. 2010. *The Cambridge Companion to Francis of Assisi*. Cambridge: Cambridge University Press.

Cantini, Gustavo. 1934. "De praedicatorum institutione et formatione in Ordine Minorum," *Acta Ordinis Fratrum Minorum* 53: 35–43.

Carta, Francesco. 2022. *Interpretare Francesco i frati, i papi e i commenti alla Regola minoritica (secc. XIII-XVI)*. Rome: Viella.

Cevins, Marie-Madeleine. 2008. *Les Franciscains observants hongrois de l'expansion à la débâcle (vers 1450-vers 1540)*. Rome, 2008.

Chardonnens, László and Bryan, Carella. eds. 2012. *Secular Learning in Anglo-Saxon England: Exploring the Vernacular*. Amsterdam: Rodopi.

Checcoli, Ippolita. 2013. "The 'Vitae' of Leading Italian Preachers of the Franciscan Observance: Fifteenth and Sixteenth-Century Hagiographical Constructions." *Franciscan Studies* 71: 281–95.

Coleman, Janet. 1991. "The Dominican Political Theory of John of Paris in its Context." *Studies in Church History*. *Subsidia* 9: 187–223.

Condren, Conal. 1977. "Marsilius of Padua's Argument from Authority: A Survey of Its Significance in the Defensor Pacis." *Political Theory* 5: 205–18.

Cooper, Donal. 2006. "Franciscan Choir Enclosures and the Function of Double-Sided Altarpieces in Pre-Tridentine Umbria." *Journal of the Warburg and Courtauld Institutes* 69: 1–54.

Copeland, Rita. 1991. *Rhetoric, Hermeneutics, and Translation in the Middle Ages: Academic Traditions and Vernacular Texts*. Cambridge: Cambridge University Press.

Davenport, Tony. 2004. *Medieval Narrative. An Introduction.* Oxford: Oxford University Press.

Debby, Nirit. 2001. *Renaissance Florence in the Rhetoric of Two Popular Preachers: Giovanni Dominici (1356-1419) and Bernardino da Siena (1380-1444)*. Turnhout: Brepols.

Debby, Nirit. 2014. *The Renaissance Pulpit: Art and Preaching in Tuscany, 1400-1550*. Turnhout: Brepols.

Deichstetter, Georg, ed. 1982. *Caritas Pirckheimer: Ordensfrau und Humanistin-ein Vorbildfur Okumene. Festschrift zum 450.Todestag*. Cologne: Wienand.

Delcorno, Carlo. 1980. "L'«ars Praedicandi» di Bernardino da Siena." *Lettere Italiane* 32: 441–75.

Delcorno, Carlo. 2000. "Medieval Preaching in Italy (1200-1500)." In *The Sermon*, edited by Beverly Mayne Kienzle, 449–560. Turnhout: Brepols.

Delcorno, Pietro. 2015. "'Quomodo discet sine docente?' Observant Efforts towards Education and Pastoral Care." In *A Companion to Observant Reform in the Late Middle Ages and Beyond*, edited by James Mixson and Bert Roest, 145–184. Leiden: Brill.

Delcorno, Pietro. 2023. "An Amphibious Identity: Apollonio Bianchi between Observance and Humanism." In *Observant Reforms and Cultural Production in Europe: Learning, Liturgy and Spiritual Practice*, edited by Pietro Delcorno and Bert Roest, 55–72. Nijmegen: Radboud University Press.

Dipple, Geoffrey. 2006. *Antifraternalism and Anticlericalism in the German Reformation: Johann Eberlin von Günzburg and the Campaign against the Friars*. Aldershot: Ashgate.

Duffy, Eduard. 2006. *The Stripping of the Altars: Traditional Religion in England, 1400-1580*. New Haven: Yale University Press.

Duggan, Lawrence. 1978. "Unresponsiveness of the Late Medieval Church: A Reconsideration." *The Sixteenth Century Journal* 9: 3–26.

Dumitrescu, Irina. 2018. *The Experience of Education in Anglo-Saxon Literature*. Cambridge: Cambridge University Press.

Graeme, Dunphy. 2010. *Encyclopedia of Medieval Chronicles*, 2 volumes. Leiden: Brill.

Edelheit, Amos. 2008. *Ficino, Pico and Savonarola: The Evolution of Humanist Theology 1461/2-1498*. Leiden: Brill.

Elm, Kaspar. 2001. "Riforme e osservanze nel XIV e XV secolo: una sinossi." In *Ordini religiosi e società politica in Italia e Germania nei secoli XIV e XV*, edited by Giorgio Chittolini and Kaspar Elm, 489–504. Bologna: Il Mulino.

Epstein, S. R. 1993. "Town and Country: Economy and Institutions in Late Medieval Italy." *The Economic History Review* 46, no. 3: 453–77.

Favier, Jean. 1966. *Les Finances pontificales à l'époque du grand schisme d'Occident, 1378-1409*. Paris: de Boccard.

Frakes, Jerold. 2011. *Vernacular and Latin Literary Discourses of the Muslim Other in Medieval Germany*. New York: Palgrave Macmillan.

Hamm, Berndt. 2004. *The Reformation of Faith in the Context of Late Medieval Theology and Piety: Essays by Berndt Hamm*. Leiden: Brill.

Henderson, John. 1994. *Piety and Charity in Late Medieval Florence*. Chicago: University of Chicago Press.

Herlihy, David. 1997. *The Black Death and the Transformation of the West*. Cambridge MA: Harvard University Press.

Hlaváček, Petr. 2005. *Čeští františkáni na přelomu středověku a novověku*. Prague: Academia.

Hofer, Johannes. 1965. *Johannes Kapistran: Ein Leben im Kampf um die Reform der Kirche*. Heidelberg: F.H.Kerle.

Housley, Norman. 1992. *The Later Crusades, 1274-1580: From Lyons to Alcazar*. Oxford: Oxford University Press.

Housley, Norman. 2004. "Giovanni da Capistrano and the Crusade of 1456." In *Crusading in the Fifteenth Century* edited by Norman Housley, 94–113. London: Palgrave Macmillan.

Housley, Norman. 2013. *Crusading and the Ottoman Threat, 1453-1505*. Oxford: Oxford University Press.

Hudson, Anne. 1988. *The Premature Reformation: Wycliffite Texts and Lollard History*. Oxford: Oxford University Press.

Huijbers, Anne. 2018. *Zealots for Souls: Dominican Narratives of Self-Understanding during Observant Reforms, c. 1388-1517*, Berlin: De Gruyter.

Imhoff, Christoph, and Deichstetter, Georg. *Caritas Pirckheimer und die Reformation in Nürnberg*. Nuremberg: Albert Hofmann, 1982.

Irwin, Thomas. 2005. "Do Virtues Conflict? Aquinas's Answer". In *Virtue Ethics, Old and New*, edited by Stephen M. Gardiner, 60–78. Ithaca: Cornell University Press.

Izbicki, Thomas. 2008a. *Reform, Ecclesiology, and the Christian Life in the Late Middle Ages*. London: Routledge.

Izbicki, Thomas. 2008b. *Reject Aeneas, Accept Pius: Selected Letters of Aeneas Sylvius Piccolomini (Pope Pius II)*. Washington, D.C.: Catholic University of America Press.

Izbicki, Thomas 2009. "The Authority of Peter and Paul: The Use of Biblical Authority During the Great Schism". In *A Companion to the Great Western Schism (1378-1417)*, edited by Joelle Rollo-Koster and Thomas Izbicki, 375–393. Leiden: Brill.

Kalous, Antonín and Stejskal, Jan (2020). "The Image of John of Capistrano in Bohemia and Moravia." In *The Mission of John of Capistrano and the Process of Europe Making in the 15th Century*, edited by Letizia Pellegrini. Rome.

Kilcullen, John. 1993. "Natural Law and Will in Ockham" *History of Philosophy Quarterly* 8: 102–127.

Kist, Johannes. 1948. *Charitas Pirckheimer: Ein Frauenleben im Zeitalter des Humanismus und der Reformation.* Bamberg: Meisenbach.

Krabbel, Gerta. 1982. *Caritas Pirckheimer: Ein Lebensbild aus der Zeit der Reformation.* Münster: Aschendorff.

Kras, Pavel and Mixson, James. 2018. *The Grand Tour of John of Capistrano in Central and Eastern Europe (1451-1456).* Lublin: Polish Academy of Science, 2018.

Lambertini, Roberto. 2005. "Poverty and Power: Franciscans in Later Medieval Political Thought." In *Moral Philosophy on the Threshold of Modernity* edited by Jill Kraye and Risto Saarinen, 141–164. Dordrecht: Springer.

Langer, Pavla. 2017. "Giovanni of Capestrano as Novus Bernardinus. An Attempt in Iconography and Relics." *Franciscan Studies* 75: 175–208.

Lappin, Anthony. 2011. "From Osma to Bologna, from Canons to Friars, from the Preaching to the Preachers: The Dominican Path Towards Mendicancy." In *The Origin, Development, and Refinement of Medieval Religious Mendicancies*, edited by Donald Prudlo, 31–58. Leiden: Brill.

Lappin, Anthony. 2011. "The Mirror of Simple Souls: Margaret Porette and the Origins of the Observant Reform." *Journal of Medieval History* 37: 329–344.

Lappin, Clare. 2000. *The Mirror of the Observance: Image, Ideal and Identity in Observant Franciscan Literature, c. 1415-1528*. Doctoral Thesis, University of Edinburgh.

Leonte, Florin. 2023. "Letters in Late Medieval Franciscan Observant Chronicles: Communication, Narrative, and Reform." *Kultúrne dejiny* 14: 249–273.

Lerner, Robert E. 1981. "The Black Death and Western European Eschatological Mentalities." *The American Historical Review* 86: 533–52.

Little, Lester. 1978. *Religious Poverty and the Profit Economy in Medieval Europe*. Ithaca: Cornell University Press.

Loose, Wilhelm. 1870. *Aus dem Leben der Charitas Pirckheimer, Abtissin zu St. Clara in Nürnberg*. Dresden: C. Heinrich.

Maschek, Hermann. 1935. "Zur Geschichte des Humanismus im Franziskanerorden." *Archivum Franciscanum Historicum* 28: 574–79.

Maurer, Wilhelm. 1971. "Humanismus und Reformation im *Nürnberg*." *Jahrbuch für frankische Landesforschung* 31: 19–34.

Meersseman, Giles. 1977. *Ordo Fraternitatis: Confraternite e pietà dei laici nel Medioevo*. Roma: Herder.

Menache, Sophia and Jeannine Horowitz. 1996. "Rhetoric and Its Practice in Medieval Sermons." *Historical Reflections/ Réflexions Historiques* 22: 321–50.

Merlo, Giovanni Grado. 2003. *Nel nome di san Francesco: Storia dei frati Minori e del francescanesimo sino agli inizi del XVI secolo*. Padova: Editrici Francescane.

Merlo, Giovanni Grado. 2012. "Franciscan Observance Between Innovation and Restoration." In *The Cambridge Companion to Francis of Assisi*, edited by Michael J. P. Robson, 139–55. Cambridge: Cambridge University Press.

Mixson, James. 2009. *Poverty's Proprietors: Ownership and Mortal Sin at the Origins of the Observant Movement*. Leiden: Brill.

Mixson, James 2015a. "Franciscan Reform and Religious Identity in Late Medieval Italy." In *Art and Identity in the Late Medieval Cistercian Monastery* edited by M. E. Cornelison. Turnhout: Brepols, 19–36.

Mixson, James. 2015b. "Observant Reform's Conceptual Frameworks between Principle and Practice". In *A Companion to Observant Reform in the Late Middle Ages and Beyond* edited by James Mixson and Bert Roest. Leiden: Brill, 60–84.

Mixson, James. 2016a. "John of Capistrano's Preaching Tour North of the Alps (1451-1456)". In *Religious Life between Jerusalem, the Desert, and the World*, edited by Kaspar Elm and James Mixson. Leiden: Brill, 255–276.

Mixson, James. 2016b. "Restricted Access Mendicants and Humanists in Florence in the Fourteenth and Fifteenth Centuries: The Problem of Justifying Humanistic Studies in the Mendicant Orders". In *Religious Life between Jerusalem, the Desert, and the World* edited by Kaspar Elm and James Mixson. Leiden: Brill, 111–137.

Moorman, John. 1968. *A History of the Franciscan Order: From Its Origins to the Year 1517*. Oxford University Press.

More, Alison. 2015. "Dynamics of Regulation, Innovation, and Invention". In *A Companion to Observant Reform in the Late Middle Ages and Beyond* edited by James Mixson and Bert Roest. Leiden: Brill, 85–110.

Mormando, Franco. 1998. "Bernardino of Siena, 'Great Defender' or 'Merciless Betrayer' of Women?" *Italica* 75: 22–40.

Mormando, Franco. 1999. *The Preacher's Demons Bernardino of Siena and the Social Underworld of Early Renaissance Italy.* Chicago: University of Chicago Press.

Muessig, Carolyn, ed. 2002. *Preacher, Sermon and Audience in the Middle Ages.* Leiden: Brill.

Muessig, Carolyn. 2015. "Bernardino da Siena and Observant Preaching as a Vehicle for Religious Transformation". In *A Companion to Observant Reform in the Late Middle Ages and Beyond* edited by James Mixson and Bert Roest, 185–203. Leiden: Brill.

Munch, Ernst. 1826. *Charitas Pirckheimer, ihre Schwestern und Nichten.* Nuremberg: Friedrich Campe.

Murphy, James. 1989. "Sermon Theory: Ars praedicandi." In *Medieval Rhetoric: A Select Bibliography* edited by James Murphy, 136–56. Toronto: University of Toronto Press.

Musco, Alessandro. 2013. *I Francescani e la politica (secc. XIII-XVII): Atti del Convegno internazionale di studio, Palermo, 3-7 dicembre 2002.* Palermo: Officina di Studi Medievali.

Navone John. 1994. "Pre-Renaissance Franciscan and Tuscan Humanism." *New Blackfriars* 75: 266–78.

Nederman, Cary J. 1995. *Community and Consent: The Secular Political Theory of Marsiglio of Padua's Defensor Pacis.* London: Rowman & Littlefield.

Nederman, Cary J. 1996. "The Meaning of "Aristotelianism" in Medieval Moral and Political Thought." *Journal of the History of Ideas* 57: 563–85.

Nelson, L. H. 1996. *The Formation of Christendom.* Oxford: Wiley-Blackwell.

Nicol, Donald M. 1993. *The Last Centuries of Byzantium, 1261-1453.* Cambridge: Cambridge University Press.

Nimmo, Duncan. 1977. "Reform at the council of Constance: the Franciscan case." *Studies in Church History* 14: 159–73.

Nimmo, Duncan. 1987. *Reform and Division in the Medieval Franciscan Order: From Saint Francis to the Foundation of the Capuchins.* Rome: Capuchin Historical Institute.

Norman, Corrie. 2003. "The Social History of Preaching: Italy". In *Preachers and People in the Reformations and Early Modern Period*, edited by Larissa Taylor. Leiden: Brill, 125–91.
Nyhus, Paul. 1975. "The Franciscans in South Germany, 1400-1530: Reform and Revolution." *Transactions of the American Philosophical Society* 65: 5–43.
Özcan, Altay. 2013. "Bartholomaeus De Jano'nun Türklerle İlgili 1438 Tarihli Bir Mektubu". *Tarih Dergisi*, 55: 81–106.
Pellegrini, Letizia. 2011. "Mendicant Friars and the Secular Clergy: From Competition to Collaboration in Pastoral Care." In *The Origin, Development, and Refinement of Medieval Religious Mendicancies*, edited by Donald Prudlo, 301–25. Leiden: Brill.
Pellegrini, Letizia. 2018. "An irreducible plural: Franciscan observances in Europe (15th century)." In *Mélanges de l'École française de Rome - Moyen Âge* [Online], 2018, retrieved on 02 January 2025. URL: http://journals.openedition.org/mefrm/4515.
Pellegrini, Letizia. 2021. *Bernardino Aquilano e la sua cronaca dell'osservanza*. Milan: Biblioteca Francescana.
Pellegrini, Letizia, and Ludovic Viallet. 2017. "Between Christianitas and Europe: Giovanni of Capestrano as an Historical Issue." *Franciscan Studies* 75: 5–26.
Phillips, Margaret. 2009. *Erasmus on His Times: A Shortened Version of the 'Adages' of Erasmus*. Cambridge: Cambridge University Press.
Pohl, Benjamin. 2023. *Abbatial Authority and the Writing of History in the Middle Ages*. Oxford: Oxford University Press.
Polecritti, Cynthia. 2000. *Preaching Peace in Renaissance Italy: Bernardino of Siena and His Audience*. Washington, D.C.: Catholic University of America Press.
Power, Amanda. 2015. "Encounters in the Ruins: Latin Captives, Franciscan Friars and the Dangers of Religious Plurality in the Early Mongol Empire." *Studies in Church History* 51: 115–36.
Rhodes, Dennis. 2011. *Studies in Early European Printing and Book Collecting*. London: Pindar Press.
Rice, Eugene. 1985. *Saint Jerome in the Renaissance*. Baltimore: Johns Hopkins University Press.
Roest, Bert. 1997. "Compilation as Theme and Praxis in Franciscan Universal Chronicles." In *Pre-modern encyclopaedic texts*, edited by Peter Binkley, 213–25. Leiden: Brill.
Roest, Bert. 2000. *A History of Franciscan Education (c. 1210-1517)*. Leiden: Brill.

Roest, Bert. 2004. *Franciscan Literature of Religious Instruction Before the Council of Trent*. Leiden: Brill.

Roest, Bert. 2014. *Franciscan Learning, Preaching and Mission c. 1220-1650*, Leiden: Brill.

Rollo-Koster, Joelle, and Izbicki, Thomas eds. 2009. *A Companion to the Great Western Schism (1378-1417)*. Leiden: Brill.

Romagnoli, Alessandra. 2011. "La Cronaca di Bernardino Aquilano: dai piccoli santi dell'Umbria alla grande Osservanza". In *Amicitiae sensibus. Studi in onore di don Mario Sensi*, edited by Alessandra Romagnoli and Fortunato Frezza, 91–124. Foligno.

Rothenhausler, Konrad. 1884. *Standhaftigkeit der altwürttembergischen Klosterfrauen im Reformationszeitalter*. Stuttgart: Verlag der Aktien-Gesellschaft.

Rubin, Miri. 1991. *Corpus Christi: The Eucharist in Late Medieval Culture*. Cambridge: Cambridge University Press.

Sanders, Julie. 2015. *Adaptation and Appropriation*. London: Routledge.

Schlemmer, Karl. 1982. *Die frommen Nürnberger und die Abtissin von St. Klara. Nürnberg als religiose Stadt in der Lebenszeit der Caritas Pirckheimer*. Nuremberg: Vier-Turme.

Şenocak, Neslihan. 2012. *The Poor and the Perfect: The Rise of Learning in the Franciscan Order, 1209-1310*. Ithaca: Cornell University Press.

Seton, Walter. 1923. *Nicholas Glassberger and His Works*. Manchester: Manchester University Press.

Silberer, Leonie. 2014. "Medieval Monastic Architecture of the Franciscan Order. Friaries as Evidence of Written and Unwritten Rules and Ideal Perceptions." In *Rules and Observance: Devising Forms of Communal Life*, edited by Mirko Breitenstein, 281–94. Berlin-Münster: LIT Verlag.

Spitz, Lewis. 1957. *Conrad Celtis the German Arch-Humanist*. Cambridge, MA: Harvard University Press.

Stinger, Charles. 1994. *The Renaissance in Rome*. Bloomington: Indiana University Press.

Stump, Philip. (2024). "From Pisa to Constance." In *Conciliar Diplomacy at the Council of Constance (1414-1418)*, edited by Philip Stump, 22–51. Leiden: Brill.

Terpstra, Nicholas. 1995. *Lay Confraternities and Civic Religion in Renaissance Bologna*. Cambridge: Cambridge University Press.

Todeschini, Giacomo. 2004. *Ricchezza francescana: Dalla povertà volontaria alla società di mercato*. Bologna: Il Mulino.

Tognetti, Giampaolo. 2013. "Preaching and Political Legitimation in Fifteenth-Century Italy: The Case of Observant Franciscan Michele Carcano." In *Preaching and Political Society: From Late Antiquity to the End of the Middle Ages*, edited by Franco Morenzoni, 299–316. Turnhout: Brepols.

Tolan, John (ed.). 2000. *Medieval Christian Perceptions of Islam*. New York: Columbia University Press.

Tolan, John. 2002. *Saracens. Islam in the Medieval European Imagination*. New York: Columbia University Press.

Tsougarakis, Nikiphoros I. 2018. "Heretical Networks between East and West: The Case of the Fraticelli." *Journal of Medieval History* 44 (5): 529–42.

Uribe, Angel and Lejarza, Fidel. 1958. *Introducción a los orígenes de la Observancia en España. Las reformas de los siglos XIV y XV*. Madrid: Archivo Ibero-Americano.

Vargas, Michael. 2016. *Taming a Brood of Vipers: Conflict and Change in Fourteenth-Century Dominican Convents*. Leiden: Brill.

Vauchez, André. 1993. *The Laity in the Middle Ages: Religious Beliefs and Devotional Practices*. Notre Dame: University of Notre Dame Press.

Viallet, Ludovic. 2013. "Social Control, Regular Observance and Identity of a Religious Order: A Franciscan Interpretation of the Libellus ad Leonem." *Franciscan Studies*, 71: 33–51.

Viallet, Ludovic. 2014. *Les sens de l'observance. Enquête sur les réformes franciscaines entre l'Elbe et l'Oder, de Capistran à Luther (vers 1450-vers 1520)*. Münster: LIT Verlag.

Viallet, Ludovic. 2016a. "Colette of Corbie and the Franciscan Reforms: The observantia in the First Half of the Fifteenth Century". In *A Companion to Colette of Corbie* edited by Joan Mueller and Nancy Warren, 65–89. Leiden: Brill.

Viallet, Ludovic. 2016b. "The Name of God, the Name of Saints, the Name of the Order: Reflections on the 'Franciscan' Identity during the Observant Period." In *Religious orders and religious identity formation, ca. 1420-1620: discourses and strategies of observance and pastoral engagement*, edited by Bert Roest and Johanneke Uphoff, 172–190. Leiden: Brill.

Weinstein, David. 1958. "Savonarola, Florence, and the Millenarian Tradition." *Church History* 27: 291–305.

Wiesner, Merry. 1992. "Ideology Meets the Empire: Reformed Convents and the Reformation." In *Germania Illustrata: Essays on Early Modern Germany Presented to Gerald Strauss*, edited by Andrew Fix and Susan Karant-Nunn, 79–98. Kirksville: Alpha.

Wilks Michael. 1977. "Alan of Lille and the New Man." *Studies in Church History* 14:137–157.

Wójcik, Rafał. 2009. "On Five Versified Mnemonic Catalogues of Popes, Emperors, and Polish Kings from the Turn of the 15th and 16th Century." In *The Charm of a List: From the Sumerians to Computerised Data Processing*, edited by Lucie Doležalová, 127–138. Newcastle upon Tyne: Cambridge Scholars Publishing.

Zaffarana, Melina. 1976. "Bernardino nella storia della predicazione populare." In *Bernardino predicatore nella società del suo tempo: XVI Convegno internazionale di studi*, 39–70. Spoleto: Accademia Tudertina.

Zarri, Gabriella. 2015. "Ecclesiastical Institutions and Religious Life in the Observant Century". *In A Companion to Observant Reform in the Late Middle Ages and Beyond* edited by James Mixson and Bert Roest, 21–59. Leiden: Brill.